Serving Time Too

Serving Time Too

A Memoir of My Son's Prison Years

Rosalind Boone Williams
with Patricia Dunlavy Valenti

Hamilton Books

Lanham • Boulder • New York • Toronto • London

Published by Hamilton Books
An imprint of The Rowman & Littlefield Publishing Group, Inc.
4501 Forbes Boulevard, Suite 200, Lanham, Maryland 20706
Hamilton Books Acquisitions Department (301) 459-3366

6 Tinworth Street, London SE11 5AL

Cover art by Matthew Wilson

British Library Cataloguing in Publication Information Available

Library of Congress Control Number: 2019936906

ISBN 978-0-7618-7147-7
ISBN 978-0-7618-7148-4

∞™ The paper used in this publication meets the minimum requirements of American National Standard for Information Sciences Permanence of Paper for Printed Library Materials, ANSI/NISO Z39.48-1992.

Printed in the United States of America

To my son, Marell, my first experience of the joy of a mother's love. I have kept my promise that your life would not be in vain, and I will always love you; and to my grandmother, Claudia McKoy, who encouraged me from her deathbed to write my book. I did it, Grandma!

"Remember the prisoners as if chained with them. . . ." Hebrews 13:3

Contents

I

Visiting the Jail
February 4, 1996, to October 9, 1997

ONE

That Night

It had been snowing, and Fayetteville, North Carolina, doesn't handle snow well. Our weather normally isn't like this, and people were having trouble driving. But we all drove to grocery stores to get bread and milk, just in case we couldn't leave home for days.

I liked the idea of being home with my children for the weekend and began roasting a turkey to take to work on Monday. This was to be one of the meals I prepared about twice a month for kids at J. S. Spivey Recreation Center, where I was the assistant director. I took pride in helping young people have fun and steer clear of trouble when they were not in school. If a child showed up on a Saturday morning at 7:30 with matted hair, a dirty face, and no breakfast, I'd want to know why. I got involved with the families and tried to touch everyone with whatever good I could do. But no one would be showing up this Saturday, and I began to wonder if the center would open again on Monday, what with all the snow. Even still, I was roasting that turkey. The oven was running and warmed the kitchen. Our house felt cozy.

My four-and-half year old, Sidnee, played at making cookies. My older daughter, Rikesia-or Kesia, as we called her at home-was a junior in high school, and she used the day to do some extra studying. My son, Marell, spent a lot of time on the phone and coming in and out of the kitchen. He snacked all day whenever he was home, and he never missed any meals, yet he was a thin 5'11". He had started growing his hair out into little plaits, and I let this slide, but I never allowed the ear piercing or tattoos he hinted about getting.

In the next few months, there would be changes that he'd have to adapt to because he had signed up to join the navy after graduation from high school. He had just turned nineteen, but he still needed my permission for some things. If he wanted to leave the house, he'd have to ask,

3

and when he asked that afternoon, I said, "No." The weather was bad and expected to get worse.

With all this snow, we were surprised when the Sawyer brothers, one after the other, showed up at our door. They lived in our neighborhood and went to school with Marell. The older brother, Tim, had been to our house before. But the younger brother, Andre, had not. I was concerned about him because he was crying hard, as I could see from the kitchen when Marell led both brothers to his room. I couldn't hear all of their conversation, but there were parts of it that made me uneasy.

In a few minutes, Marell came to the kitchen and asked if he could go with the brothers to visit Phillip. He also lived in the neighborhood and went to school with my son, and I knew him well because he was Marell's best friend and spent a lot of time in our home. On any other day I would have said, "Yes." But that day, again I said, "No." With the snow picking up, I thought Marell would be better off staying home.

But my husband saw no harm in it. James knew that Marell would probably walk over to his girlfriend's house too, and that would be fine, as long as he got back by curfew. "I mean it Marell, before 11:00," I said. But before he left, I pulled him aside and asked why that Sawyer boy had been crying. Family issues, abusive situation in the home, Marell said.

Back then before everyone had a cell phone, my son always carried a pager so that I could check in with him while he was out. When the snow started accumulating, I started worrying, and I paged him. He called from his girlfriend's house. "I'm okay," he said, "I'll be home soon."

Then at 8:00, the phone rang again. This time it was my niece who lived a few houses away. "Aunt Rosalind, have you heard about what happened? The man up the street has been shot." That man was Mr. Ed Sawyer, the father of the boys who had been in our house just that afternoon.

My mind raced for an explanation, and a thought flashed: Marell didn't know that his friends' father had been shot. If he knew, he would have certainly have called me. So I paged him and he called immediately.

"Have you heard what happened?" I asked.

"What?" he asked back.

"Your cousin called and said somebody shot Mr. Sawyer."

"No, Ma. No, no, Ma!" Marell shouted. He sounded shocked, disbelieving, and wanted to know exactly what happened. So I hung up and called my niece to find out. I thought that by now she might know something more, and she told me that it was a drive-by shooting. Mr. Sawyer was dead. As soon as I hung up the phone with her, Marell called again. He was still at his girlfriend's house.

"The man is dead," I told my son.

"No, Ma!" Marell screamed, "No, Ma! No, no!"

I really wanted my son home, although he assured me he was okay where he was. But my mind was also occupied about something that I could not control. Those Sawyer boys. I was feeling bad for them and hoping that nothing had really happened to their father, that there was some mistake in what my niece had said. So before I hung up with Marell, I asked, "Have you seen the brothers?"

"No, ma'am," he answered.

Sometimes when things go so strange and wrong, I find myself doing ordinary things as if it was an ordinary day. So that night, I prepared grape Kool-Aid for Marell as I had since he was a child. I wanted to do a little something extra to show him how much he was loved. For a few months he'd been withdrawn and a little distant, possibly because he was planning to leave home in June. I also put a Snickers Bar in his bedroom as a little surprise.

Marell arrived home on time, even a little before curfew, but instead of going right to his bedroom as usual, he stayed with James and me in the living room where we all watched television.

"Are you okay?" I asked. "Do you think the brothers would've shot their dad?"

"They wouldn't hurt a fly," Marell said. It was after midnight before he went to his room.

"Seems he didn't want to leave us," James said. Then we went to bed and tried to get some sleep.

At 5:40 in the morning we awoke with a *bang, bang, bang, bang* on the front door. James and I jumped out of bed. Our hearts pounding, we ran from the bedroom into the hall while we heard the *ring, ring, ring, ring* of the doorbell. Kesia beat her father to the front door. She was up and getting ready for her weekend job at the Waffle House. But James kept the door closed while he yelled, "Who is it? Who is it?"

"Fayetteville Police," shouted a voice from outside. Kesia opened the door, and there were two uniformed policemen and a plain-clothes detective. Detective Jason Sutherland introduced himself, and one of the men asked for Marell Williams.

"He's my son," I said, "What do you want with him?"

"We want to question him about a matter."

"What matter? What matter?"

"We want to take him to the police station for questioning about a murder in your neighborhood," Detective Sutherland said. Then he looked at James: "Sir, can you get him up? We have already talked with Phillip Brown." While James walked down the hall to get Marell, two officers stayed in the living room and the detective stayed at the entrance to the hall until James returned with our son.

He was cooperative, and one of the officers told us that we didn't have to come with him, nor did he need a lawyer. "I'm all right. I'm all right," Marell said.

Perhaps Marell could help the police, we thought. Perhaps he knew something. If Phillip had given some information, Marell might also help the police find Mr. Sawyer's murderer. James watched out the door as the officers took Marell away. They seemed so calm and concerned about his best interest. "We'll bring him back," they said.

Later, Kesia said she had seen police waiting for Marell to come out, and next day she saw their footprints in the snow forming a circle around the house. And then I questioned our parenthood, as I would for years to come. What were we thinking? Who does this? Who lets a child, even if he is legally an adult, leave with police? Were we out of our minds?

It's not that we walked around entirely trusting the police. Just a few weeks before, Kesia had an experience while driving to my grandmother's house. She had been stopped by an officer patrolling the neighborhood. He explained that it was a routine stop and asked to search her car, which she allowed him to do.

When she shared this incident with me and Marell, he spoke up: "You didn't have to let him go into the car. You have rights, and they have to have reasonable cause." I agreed and told her in the future to let police know she was aware of procedures. "Yeah," said Marell, "Next time, tell them 'No.' They would not have done that with me."

Even still, on that morning of February 4, 1996, he got into a police car and went to the station.

I have difficulty recalling what happened, or what I thought or felt during the next two hours, though I do remember that Kesia's co-worker drove her to work at the Waffle House. My head was spinning with confusion. Why would policemen want to question Marell about a neighbor's death? And I was worried about Kesia being out on dangerous, slick roads. The weather had turned so bad that churches had called off Sunday services. At least little Sidnee was still sound asleep, just like normal.

Then, at 8:20, the phone rang. It was a Detective Robert Fulmore, a man I hadn't spoken to before. "We want to let you know we have arrested Marell for first degree murder."

Now, all these years later, I still remember screaming and screaming, and through my screams, hearing the detective say, "Ma'am calm down. We've talked to him; he has confessed."

"Confessed? No, no! I want to talk to him."

James grabbed the phone, "What proof do you have? How do you know?"

"We have it from his mouth. He pulled the trigger," Detective Fulmore said.

My body sank to the floor. All I could do was lie there and sob. James woke Sidnee and brought her to my mother-in-law, and then he went to the Waffle House. Kesia needed to come home now, to be with us. James wanted to tell her about Marell before she heard it from anyone else.

When the doorbell rang at 9:30, I couldn't move or speak. I had no idea who it was. The doorbell rang again. I was sobbing, but I managed to say, "Who is it?"

"Mrs. Williams, this is the police. We have your son with us."

I was so shocked I couldn't stand to open the door. I wanted to see Marell, to hug him, but dread and fear and denial kept me lying on the floor, crying, "No, no, no."

"Ma'am, if you just let us in, you'll be able to see your son."

I had no strength to get up, but I dragged myself to the door and opened it a little. Marell was standing there with Detective Fulmore and another officer. My son seemed powerless, and his face was full of sadness.

"Ma'am, please let us in. We have prayed with Marell, and we thought that you'd want to pray with him too." I thought to myself: "God has a hand in this if the police bring my son home to pray with me." The detective's words helped me to find the strength to stand and let them in. At that very moment, James and Kesia arrived. We all stood in a circle in the living room, the detective too, and prayed. James led the prayer. I do not remember the words now, but I do remember that I held on to my belief that God was in control. Then I hugged Marell, and he began to cry on my shoulder.

I whispered in his ear, "Did you shoot this man?"

"No, ma'am," he whispered.

The life that I had known, all that I had built and hoped for ended that day. My new life had begun.

TWO

Looking Back

I thought Detective Fulmore had been kind to bring Marell home and to pray with us, but weeks later, Marell told me that this was part the detective's plan to recover the murder weapon. He had promised Marell that he could see his family before being taken to jail only if he took the police to the gun that shot Mr. Sawyer. To this day, I don't know if Marell took them to the gun before or after we prayed. This is one of many questions I will never have answered.

I felt so powerless, confused. Why would Marell have confessed? Why would he kill this man? This confession must be a mistake. I had to see my son, to get everything cleared up. All that morning, I called the jail, talking to one after another person to learn how we could visit Marell even though James said the roads were too bad to leave the house. I didn't care about slick roads. We had to see Marell that day. Because James could not bear to see me cry, he agreed to risk the drive.

But before going to the jail, we drove the three blocks to Marell's girlfriend's house. Cheryl is what I'll call her here, for she has gone on to make a decent life for herself, and she should not be known because of her past associations or mistakes. And Marell's best friend, the brothers, their parents—I'm not using their real names either. Despite the pain they have caused me, they have felt pain, too. Out of respect for that, I won't call them by name.

Even though Cheryl was younger than Marell, she was streetwise, and I thought she might know something that would help me clear him. I knew that some people living in her home did drugs. The mother in me did not like Marell spending so much time in that home, even if I had no reason to think anything bad about Cheryl, and I didn't want to blame her for having to live with those people.

Sure enough, Cheryl knew plenty about what had happened, but I was not prepared for what she told me and James. She explained that Marell had gotten a gun for Mrs. Sawyer several weeks ago and had given it to her, but then she gave it back to him. Marell had told Mrs. Sawyer he did not want anything to do with it—that is, whatever *it* was that she planned to do with a gun. Whatever she wanted done, she could do herself.

I could hardly absorb what Cheryl said. This was not what I thought she might tell us, but at least with this information, we might make things better for Marell. I figured he had done something stupid; so had others, but those others were responsible for Mr. Sawyer's death.

Past events flew into my mind. I began to understand why Mrs. Sawyer had come to my house two months before. I'd never spoken to the woman, never laid eyes on her, but there she was one December day, sitting in her car parked at the curb with one of her sons. She sent him to knock on my door and say that she wanted Marell to show her where Phillip lived. I said Marell wasn't going anywhere. He was being punished for coming in after curfew. Still, the lady was hollering out the window of her car, flagging me with her hand.

"I'm going to bring him right back," she said. So I gave in. She was the mother of a boy in the neighborhood. Surely there was nothing wrong with Marell doing a favor by showing her where Phillip lived.

"Okay, Marell," I said, "But you'd better come right back." And he did.

Then two months later, on that miserable, cold February morning, there we were at Cheryl's house, listening to what she told us about Mrs. Sawyer discussing money with Marell and Phillip. Those conversations went on for weeks, Cheryl said. This was bad, I knew, much worse than I could have guessed, but nothing showed me that Marell had shot Mr. Sawyer. At the worst, he knew who did, and perhaps he made the mistake of helping to dispose of the gun.

Yes. That was it. Yes. That was how he knew where the gun was.

I've never been in an earthquake, but now I felt like I was in the middle of one. I could imagine how it would feel. There is nothing steady to stand on so you grasp at anything you can reach, and you hold on to it, even if it lets you fall. And so my understanding of what happened came in spurts. That morning I learned that Phillip had been arrested for the murder too; I heard it on TV. The next day the newspaper reported how a gun had been fired twice through the window of the Sawyers' house. One of the bullets struck Mr. Sawyer in the chest, killing him where he sat in his living room. The newspaper also reported that Wanda Sawyer had been arrested for hiring Marell and Phillip to do this. But no money had changed hands.

It seemed as if I was putting together the pieces of an ugly puzzle. And I began to see how another piece of this puzzle fit into the last few weeks of our lives. About the same time Mrs. Sawyer showed up at our house, Marell began to be moody. He and I had always been close, even when he got into scrapes, but then he stayed clear of me.

That's not unusual, I know, for seniors in high school. They want to prove they're independent, ready to move on. But because I was worried about Marell, I had made an appointment with a therapist. I knew Marell wouldn't want to go, so I told him I was the one who needed counseling, and it would help me if he came along. He could fill in information about the family. I wasn't really lying. I did need counseling and advice on how to snap Marell out of his mood. He'd be going off to the navy after graduation, and I wanted our last months together as a family to be as happy as possible.

So I had checked Marell out of school one morning, and we went to see a family therapist who worked in a small office at a counseling center not far from our home, a place that I had noticed passing through the area daily. By the time we arrived at the office, Marell had become suspicious and a little angry. He knew I'd tricked him; he was shutting down, everything about him letting us know, "I don't want to be here. Why did my mother have me come here?"

Soon the therapist asked me if I would step out of the room so he could talk to Marell alone. Not even ten minutes went by when the therapist asked me to come back. Marell had his head down and let us do the talking.

I was dealing with the typical issues, the therapist told me, not the kind of things he saw with really troubled teenagers who refused to go to school or rebelled against authority.

But there were a few incidents that had worried me. Marell had a little job that put some money in his pocket. One day he bought himself a pair of pants at J. C. Penney's and put a second pair in the bag without paying for them. He'd let bad company influence him that day, got caught, and had to face a judge in court. She had a very dignified attitude. With her deep voice that conveyed authority, she told Marell that he seemed like a smart young man who was lucky to have loving, supportive parents, so she sentenced him to only sixty-five hours of community service. He successfully completed these hours in work that he loved, making props at our regional theater. He was always talented in carpentry, and the staff at the theater recognized and appreciated this. They were happy to have him, and he was happy to be there.

And there was a fight at school at the beginning of Marell's senior year. He and Phillip were accused of ganging up on another boy who was not known to be a troublemaker. Even though several students were involved, the school resource officer named only Marell and Phillip. They were hauled off to the Cumberland County Jail, arrested, and put in a holding cell right next door to the courthouse.

Lucky for Marell and Phillip, they stayed there under an hour, just long enough to get a scare. And those jokers were scared by the time James and I came to pick them up, both of them, at the courthouse. Phillip's grandmother had no car to come get him so she asked that he be released in our care. When the case came to court, a teacher and the boy who was attacked testified that Marell was not involved.

After these events, a guidance counselor at the high school, Mr. Carlton Butler, decided he needed to take some personal time with Marell. He talked with him about the direction that his life was headed and told him about programs that would challenge him to be positive and finish school. The Tarheel Challenge in Salemberg, North Carolina, about an hour's drive from our home, was this kind of program. It is a military style boot camp boarding school run by the National Guard for boys with potential but who are getting into trouble in regular public schools. The Tarheel Challenge had a lot of structure and discipline. I'd always been a big fan of structure and discipline and preached those values to my children.

The counselor made plans to travel to the Tarheel Challenge with Marell and me. I suggested that Phillip come too since both boys needed direction and motivation. The place was in the middle of nowhere on Highway 87 in eastern North Carolina and consisted of about four buildings that were not modernized at all. The participants slept in one building, studied and ate in another. The rules were very strict. Boys had no access to phone or television for the first several weeks. Lights were out at the required time with no exceptions. Because the program is federally funded, if a young man was approved for it, he would attend for free and work towards passing the GED, the General Educational Development test that was the equivalent of earning a high school diploma. After receiving a GED, he would be allowed to do job training and receive a stipend. The director explained that no one would be forced to stay and could leave at any time. But if a boy left the premises, he would not get a second chance.

On our drive back from Salemburg, Mr. Butler and I asked Marell and Phillip whether they'd like to give that boot camp a chance. Phillip said he would, but Marell grumbled that he didn't want to go there. And that was the end of it, because Phillip followed and sided with Marell.

I wasn't naïve. I knew the trouble boys get into. I had seen enough with the kids at Spivey Rec Center. And some crime trickled into our neighborhood, usually because of people who came from the streets that surround us. But most of our neighbors owned their homes-brick ranch houses that were built in the 1950s and 60s. A lot of military people had moved there after getting out of the army at Fort Bragg. That's what happened in my family, and neighbors were pretty close-knit. Kesia said they would sometimes tell on kids if they did something wrong, and at times, even Marell and his friends did get in trouble.

But I never worried about Kesia. She concentrated on being a star student at school and hung out with kids who also liked to study. She didn't get in much trouble, only in small situations when taking up for Marell. We felt she didn't need to carry a pager. We could always keep up with her whereabouts because she didn't have the run of the neighborhood. She could go to our neighborhood rec center only if she was with her brother or a female friend that we approved of.

And I didn't feel the need to check out her room from time to time like I did Marell's. The "shakedown," I called it. I'd go into his room and look in his desk and drawers and check behind the books on his shelf. Whenever there was talk of money, I needed to find out how Marell planned to get it or where it came from. I knew what I could afford to spend on his sneakers, and one day, when he came home wearing fancy, expensive sneakers, I went crazy. Oh no, not here!

"I did not buy, you do not wear," I told Marell, and I did not stop asking where the sneakers came from until he gave me a name. Plus, I called the police. A female and a male officer showed up. They kind of chuckled when I told them that I called them because my son had come in with an extra $55.00 and a new pair of shoes that his parents had not purchased. James looked a little embarrassed as I told the police they needed to take our son. It was drug money! I was sure of that. But the police said there was nothing legally to be done. They suggested that if I knew the dealer, we should return the money and shoes.

James and I immediately went to the suspected dealer's house where he lived with his grandmother. She was the only one there at the time and insisted that we were wrong about Marell's acquisition and about her grandchild. She refused the money and shoes. So I left the shoes outside her front door and went straight to the post office and used that $55.00 for a money order to pay on our house taxes. That gave me relief that my son wasn't going to be able to keep or spend drug money.

I knew a lot could go wrong with a son, and I felt that I had my share with Marell's problems. But the story had been the same with those officers as it had with the family therapist. Both the police and the therapist looked me in the eye and said I was only dealing with routine problems.

"Does he do his chores and homework?" the therapist asked.

"Yes," I answered.

"Does he cut school?" he asked.

"No, he knows better."

The therapist laughed. "You know Marell respects you. He knows what he has to deal with. You have control."

Those words should have made me comfortable. After all, this therapist had worked with young men like Marell every day and had talked to many other mothers and had seen bigger problems than the one I brought to him.

Still, when Marell and I left his office, I wondered if he was right.

THREE
That First Week

On February 4th, we were not the only people driving on ice to see someone in jail during visiting hours.

That day marks the first time I had actually been inside the Cumberland County Jail though I passed it every day when I went to work. On the first floor of this four-story beige brick building, long lines of people crowded into the lobby. We were all bundled up in coats and boots, and I would later learn about the strict dress code that was enforced on visitors. On another Sunday, a woman looked like she'd just come from church. She was nicely dressed in a suit, but the guard thought her skirt was too short and made her leave. On another occasion, I was even turned away for wearing sandals.

All these procedures were new to us that Sunday in 1996, but one of the white guards acted as if we shouldn't be there if we didn't know the rules. "This is my first time here," I said to him, but I thought to myself: "Just because you see a black mother you think this is normal for me and that I should know how things work in jail. Well, I don't." I kept silent, but my husband broke down crying and said to the man, "This is our first time here. Our son is here."

Slowly, James, Kesia, and I made progress through our line toward an elevator that held no more than eight people. Once we got to the third floor where the cells were, there was a waiting room with about twenty chairs surrounded by glass walls that were divided into little booths no more than twenty-four inches wide. The noise in that place was terrible. Everyone was shouting even the most personal things. A boyfriend and girlfriend were arguing about seeing their children. Nothing could be private. I found myself looking from one little booth to the next and becoming more and more fearful because we did not know what to expect. When I broke down, James said: "We're going to do this, we're going to do this, we are going to do this." Then, suddenly, after all our waiting, there was Marell behind the glass.

The three of us crowded together on our side of the booth and spoke to him through a little opening that looked like the kind that is found in banks. We had to bend toward it to speak one at a time. I could see that Marell had been crying. He said he had been charged with first-degree murder and conspiracy to commit murder. Phillip and Mrs. Sawyer had been charged along with him. I wanted to say something encouraging, but I was crying too hard to speak. James and Kesia managed to make small talk. But we did not know much about Marell's circumstances or the charges against him. James assured Marell that we would find out more the next day at his first appearance in court.

"I want to get out of here," Marell said over and over.

"We are going to work on it; we just have to pray," I said, holding my hands together to symbolize praying. All I had to offer was my strong faith. I could not touch my son, but every now and then, I would touch the glass, and Marell would put his hand on the other side. We had no more than ten minutes with him when a guard came up behind him, tapped his shoulder, and said, "Your time is up."

"Please, can you give me a little longer, please," I begged. I'm sure the guard had seen many mothers crying for more time.

The visit was over.

The morning of Monday, February 5th came slowly.

At about 8:00 in the morning, we called the courthouse and found out it was closed because of the snow. But James learned what would happen at Marell's first appearance in court. It would be short, just enough time for the judge to read the charges, check that the accused's name was correct, and determine if he needed a court appointed attorney. We also learned that each prisoner could have an account with as much as $40.00 deposited in it each week to buy necessities like soap, toothpaste, and shampoo. So I drove over the frozen roads to the jail and deposited some money for Marell, and I also brought him clean underwear because I was told there were no facilities in the jail for inmates to do personal laundry. How did inmates manage, I wondered, if no loved one took care of them in this basic way?

For the first time in my life, I realized that having clean underwear and brushing your teeth was a luxury, not a right.

I watched the hands of the clock tick past every hour until the morning of February 6th dawned. That morning, I was a nervous wreck trying to get dressed for court. I paced the floor while James tried to calm me down. He kept trying to comfort me, telling me that it was going to be okay.

Ice and snow were still on the ground, but court did open, and when we arrived at the courthouse, the parking lot was nearly full. Almost every space was taken. The courtroom would also be packed. James had warned me about this.

He was so worried about me. I was exhausted from lack of sleep and worry; my legs felt too weak to move, but somehow they did. I had not eaten, and I hardly drank any liquids in two days. James helped me walk and made me stop by the first water fountain. But I felt like my throat was blocked, and I couldn't swallow, so I grabbed his shirt, pulling him toward Courtroom 2C, and we walked in.

It was horrible to enter this room with the judge seated at the bench directly front and center. The witness box was on the right side, as was the court recorder. Further to the right was a glassed-in area where twelve to fourteen jailed defendants were seated, waiting for their names to be called, but Marell wasn't among them yet. In front of the judge's bench were two tables, one where the defendant would stand with his attorney, if he had one. At the other table, someone from the District Attorney's Office was overseeing a small box containing a list of the defendants' names.

There were too many people in this room; the walls seemed to be closing in. But somehow we managed to find seats, and I noticed there were at least three rows full of people who had come out of concern for Marell and our family. So many. things were running through my mind at that moment. I could hardly speak. I wanted to say and ask a lot, but the words just wouldn't come out. I was so stressed that I cannot remember all who were there, though I was told later about those who had come. I do remember seeing Cheryl and her mother, several of Marell's friends, and his football coach from our neighborhood rec center. The counselor who had come with us to visit the Carolina Challenge was there, as were family members, and my goddaughter. And there were other friends, too. They all geared their eyes on us. No one said a word. We shared our pain in silence.

In only minutes, I began to hyperventilate, and James again tried to get me to step out for water. But I dared not be caught outside when Marell was brought in. Judge Eugene Alderman had already begun the proceedings, and he was short with each person making a first appearance in court. He read the charges, made sure the defendant understood them, and asked if he-there were only men making a first appearance that day-could afford his own attorney or needed the court to appoint one. Then the judge asked them if they had any family present who would speak up for them.

Of the three people charged with Mr. Sawyer's death, Phillip was the first to appear. Judge Alderman asked if he had any family in court, and I remember for sure that his frail grandmother was present along with his basketball coach, and I think his sister might have been there too. Unlike Marell, Phillip didn't have so many relatives or friends to stand by him.

And while Phillip was making his first appearance before the judge, my mind wandered to January 14, 1977, the day that I gave birth to a bundle of joy. Marell had taken all my energy that morning. I was so weak that I could only hold him for a short time before the nurses took him away. Now I wanted to hold him just that way. I wanted to hug and kiss him.

Those memories were interrupted when the bailiff walked Marell into the courtroom and seated him in the glassed-in area. He spotted us immediately. He was in handcuffs and looked straight into my eyes, like he had when he was just six years old. Then, cookies had gone missing from the cabinet without permission, and to scare him and Kesia into owning up, I said the Social Services van would come to pick them up if they did not tell the truth. Marell cried for hours. Now, this situation was so much, much more serious. This crime could take him away for life.

My breathing got worse, so James forced me to walk out of the courtroom with him. A friend followed behind us and led me in the women's restroom. I could hardly breathe, so she yelled into the hallway for James. In no time, an EMS team was on the scene and checked my blood pressure. It was too high and the medics wanted to carry me to the hospital, but I shook my head "no." James knew what I was trying to say. The EMS attendant said that if they had to come back for me again, I would have no choice but to go to the hospital.

I hung on James's arm for strength, and together we re-entered the courtroom. Several minutes later, I heard my son's name: "Marell LaTrek Williams." With his ankles chained together, he shuffled as best he could to stand in front of the judge. It was as if a pain had stabbed my heart, and I cried out. The judge stared at me, and James whispered that I had to be calm and quiet so as not to disrupt the court. But why? How could I? That was my son.

Judge Alderman began by asking Marell to state his full name for the court. Next, he asked if Marell understood what he had been charged with. "Yes, sir," he answered. He was the seventh person that morning to answer to a murder charge. Then the judge asked if he had any family in court.

James tried to stand up to approach the bench, but I pulled on his shirt for dear life. "Don't go without me," I managed to whisper. With a friend's help, James led me to stand in front of the judge and told him that we were James and Rosalind Williams, Marell's parents.

James's voice shook as he began to speak. "Marell made a mistake . . . ," and he never finished the sentence because I raised my head and looked in the judge's eyes. I hadn't been able to talk before, but God spoke through me loud and clear: "He is our son, and we will be with him through this. And I continue to believe that I can do all things through Christ who strengthens me."

Judge Alderman then read the charges. Possibly a first-degree murder, a capital case, he said. Marell might be facing the death penalty, and then the judge asked if we had an attorney. He was directing that question to *us*, to James and to me, not just to Marell. He seemed to hint that it would be better for Marell if we could get a private attorney, but that expense was beyond us. So Marell requested and was given a court appointed attorney.

As the guards led Marell out of court, Judge Alderman said: "May God be with you." He had not spoken such heartfelt, caring words to other families. We left the courtroom with tears tagged with questions where to turn next.

By Thursday, February 8th, Marell had a court appointed attorney, Vernon Stevenson; his wife acted as his assistant and investigator. He met with Marell for the first time just briefly before meeting with James and me. Mr. Stevenson said he wanted to get a feel for Marell through his family and had done some investigating into us, and had learned that Marell was not a truant, that he maintained his grades at school-not great grades but good enough for the navy recruiter. Marell had no record of violent offense, no history of drug use. Mr. Stevenson found out only good things about Marell's home life-no abuse, and devoted, supportive parents with stable jobs, mine at the rec center and James's as a custodial supervisor for Cumberland County Schools. We were different from the families of defendants Mr. Stevenson typically dealt with, and he found nothing he could use to explain or excuse the charges against Marell. But a violent crime had taken place after the discussion of money. Those facts-a violent, planned murder, talk about the exchange of money-could make a capital case in the state of North Carolina. So from jump, the attorney let us know this was an "unusual" case. That was his exact word.

Then Mr. Stevenson mapped out what would happen. There would be bond hearings, and after he received the "discovery," the matter would go before the grand jury to decide if it was a capital case. Discovery was a term we had never heard before, so he explained the rules laid out by the law. Both the defense and prosecution had to hand over to each other any evidence that they turned up. These rules were supposed to direct both sides in their investigation of a case. Mr. Stevenson said he could make general or specific requests for evidence from the prosecution, and they were not allowed to withhold anything. As yet, they had handed nothing over to him.

We began to see that things would not go fast, but at least the ball was rolling. James and I were scheduling appointments with Mr. Stevenson, calling the navy recruiter to tell him about Marell, and listing dependable persons for character references such as the school psychologist, Marell's English tutor, and the counselor we'd seen in January-the man who said everything was okay. Mr. Stevenson planned to set Marell up with a psychologist who frequently worked for the North Carolina Department of Correction. Mrs. Stevenson would continue to investigate and question witnesses.

And we were praying and praying.

Going to church the first Sunday after Marell's arrest was difficult for me, though the Church of Christ had been my church home since I was fourteen. I had raised my children there, and Kesia and Marell along with Sidnee were accustomed to attending almost every Sunday. We always sat on the right side, up toward the front. Even though there were times James did not join us, the children knew that they must attend if they planned to do any other activities that day.

Back in February of 1996, our congregation had recently moved into a new, big building where the walls, floor, and seats are shades of green. The flowers are always a peach color that reminds me of my wedding color. The pulpit is front and center with seats slightly in back on each side of it. The communion table sits below the pulpit with "Do This In Remembrance of Me" written on it. Right behind the pulpit is the baptismal pool. When men and women come to be baptized, they dress in white gowns and step all the way into that pool of water. At services, our congregation provides a cappella singing. All this was my life at church, where I felt welcomed and loved.

I never claimed to be a perfect Christian, yet I worked hard to set a good example to my family. After Marell's arrest, I knew that I needed to go to church for Sunday service more than anything else. I kept praying, "Lord, you know I need you. Right now, I need you." But I worried how the congregation was going to react to me and the girls. A few of my close church brothers and sisters had made contact with me during the week, and of course, I'd called the minister. He had come to our home to talk and pray with us. And that Sunday, James did come with us; he assured me that we were in this together.

So we all went, and when we got there, my heart was so heavy that I didn't want to look up. But my brothers and sisters acted no different than usual toward us. A few came over and hugged me, for I cried throughout most of the service. They asked if I was okay and said they would pray for us. One of the sisters said to be sure to tell Marell that she was praying for him.

We were going to need that prayer, and more. This situation with Marell was higher than me. My faith was being tested.

FOUR

That First Month

By the end of Marell's first week in jail, our family had begun a routine, one we thought would last a few weeks, or possibly, at most, a few months. Little did we know.

Marell would call almost every night and sometimes during the day if he knew someone was home to answer. When the phone rang, we'd hope to hear a recording, "You have a collect call from Cumberland County Jail," followed by an announcement that all calls were monitored. Marell was allowed to call as often as he wanted, but because each call charged $3.80 to our phone bill, we just couldn't afford to let Marell call as often as he wanted to. A call was supposed to last ten minutes, but you best believe it never did. By the time the recorded announcement was through, we were lucky to have nine minutes.

Thursdays became the day I'd get a bundle of Marell's laundry from the guards at the jail. I'd take the laundry home, wash it, and when I came for a visit, I'd give it to the guards who'd then hand it back to Marell. It was like clockwork. I never missed a week bringing clean underwear, depositing money in Marell's account, and visiting. But besides seeing the lawyer, who could come at any time, Marell was allowed only one visit a week from up to three adults at a time. And if someone other than Marell's family came, that person would be counted as one of the visitors for the week, and I'd be denied my visit.

The staff at the jail quickly got to know me. Some of them treated me as if I was the inmate, not a grieving mother too upset to speak up quickly when my name was called. Once a guard snapped that if I didn't answer quickly and loudly, I'd lose my chance for the whole visit.

But some of the others on the staff were very kind. Several of the officers felt relaxed enough to comment to us about Marell's behavior. One female guard told me that she heard other prisoners use the "b" word all the time, but Marell never did. He was very respectful, and they wondered how he got into this terrible situation. I marveled at these comments because they reminded me of when Marell and Kesia were little. People in stores, church, or school always commented on the way they showed good manners and behaved so well. To hear jail officers say good things about Marell made me smile. They'd even tried to console me when I left the facility in tears, as I did each time I visited. I stood by the fact that Marell had a good upbringing, good heart, and good morals. But he let peer pressure consume him.

One of the kindest people at the jail was the man who ran it, Major William Whirley. He would walk through the visitors' area, friendly and courteous to the parents. When my mother came from Texas, he made it easy for her to visit Marell. She was anxious to see her first grandchild, though James and I had tried to get her to hold off. But she insisted, and having her visit Marell turned out to be a simple process, as Major Whirley explained. Mother's visit would be called a special one, he said. With her out-of-state ID, she could come during the week, have extra time, and join one other person for Marell's regular weekend visit. When my mother and I visited him together, we were both a bucket of tears, and he begged us to stop crying. Mother was able to visit several more times during that week she stayed with us, and her conversations encouraged him because she was so knowledgeable about God's word.

I had much comfort knowing that Marell had face-to-face conversations with visitors. They lifted him up most of the time; other times, they did not. He hated being in jail and had frequently asked me to inquire about bond or house release. He listened constantly to other inmates-I call them jailhouse lawyers-who had persuaded him that his situation did warrant house release. And that's just what Marell wanted to hear.

Then, on February 14th, the day of love, Marell's real lawyer called. Mr. Stevenson had some good news and some bad news. The good news was that the jail was just starting a new in-house program where the inmates could attend classes to prepare for the GED. This way they could obtain their high school diplomas since they wouldn't be graduating from high school as planned. He would talk with Major Whirley about allowing Marell to participate. The attorney also gave a few dates for hearings to determine if Marell's would be a capital case, yet Mr. Stevenson stated that Marell would not be brought into court for those hearings because the process was so short.

But Mr. Stevenson was negative about any possible bond or house release and wanted me to be the one to tell Marell. Matter of fact, Mr. Stevenson was eager to pass as many tasks off to me *as* he could, *because* he could. Most of his clients didn't have families who were eager to help in any way or get involved. He knew I would pick up loose ends and that I wouldn't stop calling and asking questions until I got answers. I was beginning to understand that helping Marell was like having a part-time job.

I dreaded to tell Marell the news about bond and house release when he called. When I did, he flipped out and said that he wanted another attorney, that Mr. Stevenson wasn't working hard enough for him. Then Marell shut down. He said he didn't even care that he might complete high school while he was in jail. He became distant, his calls fell off, and he asked that I take a break from the cards and letters that I was sending every other day. The reality of where he was hit him hard.

And I was learning just how bad the conditions were for him. Our local newspaper ran an article about all the problems in Cumberland County Jail. It had been built to hold 288 inmates, but on any day there might be as many as 340 men jailed there. Anyone over the 288-man limit didn't get a bed but instead slept on a mattress on the floor. Inmates had to step over each other to get to the bathroom, and they had no fresh air, and no recreation other than television or board games as rewards for good behavior. Guards monitored the inmates by means of cameras that were mounted in the halls of the cellblocks, but cameras didn't show what was happening inside the cells. Given these tight conditions and the lack of direct supervision, tempers flared easily. When inmates got into a fight, the staff had trouble breaking it up quickly. Around once a week, an inmate was injured so bad in a fight that he had to go to the hospital.

My heart ached when I thought about the conditions Marell lived in, especially when I went into his room at home. In 1989, our family had moved into a larger house and for the first time, Marell and Kesia each had a bedroom. Marell's bedroom was a little smaller than Kesia's, nothing elaborate, yet he did not mind. It was his, for him, all by himself. He spent a lot of time there. He called it his "chillin' space." I called it a place where it would be easier for him to concentrate on his schoolwork. I put a desk in his room so he did not even have to leave to study, and he had his own dresser and TV. He pinned sports articles and pictures from *Jet* magazine on the back of his door. But allowing my kids to stay behind closed doors was a not a regular habit that I agreed with. Only as recognition of good behavior or good grades, I sometimes allowed them to close the door to listen to music in privacy. And they were responsible for the upkeep of their rooms. That included washing their clothes and changing sheets every two weeks. Frequently, I had to remind Marell about the messiness on his desk or picking up his clothes from the bed. Even though I considered this normal for a teenage boy, he knew when I had had enough and when he needed to get on top of his chores. He became so proud of his room that he marked it with a wood sign he'd made in ninth-grade woodshop class. It read "Boone's Place," Boone recognizing my maiden name, which became his tag-along nickname.

But now Marell was telling me about the situations in the jail and how many bad fights broke out and how some inmates took other inmates' belongings. When that happened, Marell said he just turned over in his bed-he was one of the lucky ones who had a bed-and prayed for that person. Sometimes he'd go to the TV room, but mostly he'd stay in his cell by himself when cellmates left for the day to watch TV. He'd try to keep me from worrying by saying he was okay. But I did worry. He was living with men in crowded conditions who had nothing to do but get on each other's nerves. Really, how could they be expected to live in that jail without getting into worse trouble than what had brought them there?

I had always told Marell that every time he got mad at someone and wanted to fight, that someone had a family and loved ones who cared about him also (even though by now I began to realize that wasn't true for some of these inmates). These were hard words to live by, especially now. I'm sure my prayers kept Marell from getting into trouble even when he became more and more anxious to talk with the attorney. Mr. Stevenson had not seen him in weeks and a few of the court dates had been cancelled. Major Whirley had not responded yet about the high school program. Marell finally understood that he wasn't going home any time soon.

Life was not all fancy-dory outside either. Newspaper articles surfaced about Mr. Sawyer's murder and the arrests of Mrs. Sawyer, Phillip, and Marell. Kesia was directly affected by all of this. Every day she went to school with the Sawyer boys who were free to murmur whatever they wanted about her brother. Kesia had to put up with whispers from students, and even from teachers. "That's the sister of the Marell Williams who's been charged with murder," she'd hear them say. It became enough of a problem that Mr. Butler called us out of concern for Kesia's safety at school. But Kesia, well, she's tough. She somehow managed to keep up her good grades and go to work regularly at her part-time job.

And then there was the newspaper article about Phillip, headline, "Basketball Team Stunned: Athlete's Arrest Shocks Many." The article quoted people from the high school, like a coach who said Phillip was a "good person" and had "a really good heart," and his teammates, who said they were praying for him. Why did that article have to include that Phillip was a leading free-throw shooter for the team and to list his stats for rebounds and his percentage from the line? Did Phillip deserve sympathy because he was valuable to the basketball team? It sure seemed that way.

So many people had an opinion and thought they had the right to ask personal questions. "Did someone make him do it?" "And for money?" A co-worker boldly asked: "You think Marell killed that man? What was going through his mind to do such a thing?" I let her know I would not be discussing this matter with her then, or ever. Still, I became a nervous wreck and would often hide in the restroom at work or seek my bedroom at home for refuge. I ran to be alone every chance I got to shed my tears.

I began to grasp for knowledge anywhere I could. I watched every detective show on TV and movies that could shed any light on murder cases, like a movie called *Seduced by Madness*. I sat and watched it, taking notes until it was over. It was about a teacher in Wisconsin who'd hired two of her students to kill her abusive husband. I knew the circumstances were different, but they were alike in some facts. She was tried and received more time than the boys she'd hired. My imagination led me to wonder if this might help my son's case. I know now that I was grasping at straws, but I wanted something, anything, that could help me to help Marell.

When Marell finally wrote his first letter from jail on February 26th, it was to his dad. Marell expressed that when he got out, he wanted to become much closer to James. They could go fishing together, Marell wrote, regretting that before, "I guess we both were too manly to get close to each other. But when I get out of here that's one of my goals." And Marell thanked James for being such a good provider: "I see why you and Mama was always on me about responsibility. . . . I'm going to have it when I raise up outta here."

He was right. We had always been on him about responsibility. In fact, "Respect and Responsibility" were the gifts we had given him for his eighteenth birthday. We'd bought an '88 Nova that Marell could use to go back and forth to school and other approved places. But we didn't see this as giving him a car. We saw it as giving him "Respect and Responsibility," and so we had drawn up a contract with rules about how the privilege of the car was granted. He'd have to show responsibility about his schoolwork and chores and associates. "What kinda parents give their son 'Respect and Responsibility' as an eighteenth birthday present?" he joked, knowing exactly the answer. "Your kind of parents," we laughed.

By the end of February, I had found a new means of connecting with my son. I noticed that sometimes inmates would yell out from their windows to their families as they drove off after a visit. From the window in his jail cell, Marell could see our van when we pulled down the street and into the parking lot. So I began to come at dusk, often on my way home from work, and stop at the parking lot. It was well lit there, so I felt safe to get out of my van and stand beside it. Then I'd look up at a window where I knew he'd be standing. I couldn't make out his face, just the outline of his slim body, and then he'd wave a towel and call our home phone number collect. James, or more often Kesia, would answer and use a new technology we had, a "three-way." This allowed his call to connect with another new thing, my car phone, which was the size of a regular cordless phone that I kept charging in the front seat of my van. After talking to Marell this way for eight to nine minutes and seeing him at the window, I would feel all right. This became a daily routine for me. Only a few evenings did I miss because of the weather, or being sick, or when I was out of town.

I never saw any other inmate's family do this, though. I felt no embarrassment or shame about it, and I kept doing it, even after I was approached by a sheriff's deputy. He was one of those cocky men who liked to show his rank, and he advised me to stop my daily appearances in front of Marell's cell window.

"Sis," he said, "I'm trying to help you out before the white man comes to arrest you."

"What could he arrest me for?" I asked. I had committed no crime, no trespassing, no disturbance, no yelling. I was just blowing kisses and talking on the phone to my son, which was allowed.

"Can't say I didn't warn you cuz they been talking about you," he said, walking off.

Several months later, a park patrol officer with the Fayetteville Police Department, who covered the area where I worked, shared something with me he wasn't supposed to. He told me the deputies were talking about a lady who came every day in her burgundy van to stand in front of the jail so that she could see and talk to her son. They knew I was talking to an inmate, and they weren't sure how the three-way calling fit into jail rules. But they just agreed to leave me alone.

FIVE

That Spring

Marell was really missing home and his family, especially Sidnee. In addition to our three-way calls, he'd call about three to four times a week in the mornings and then again in the evenings to speak to Kesia and Sidnee. He loved both of his sisters, but the relationship with Sidnee was special because he was so much older than she was. When I was pregnant with her, he sang to her in my belly. Ever since she was able to walk, she'd traveled into Marell's room; he allowed her in when no one else could enter. Then he would close the door and pump his music and TV as loud as he thought I would allow. She would bounce up and down, singing right along with him. She loved it.

Now, when Sidnee asked for her brother, we didn't know what to say. She'd never even heard the word "jail," so we told her that he was away at school. She could understand that because twice he and Kesia had gone to educational summer camps away from home. Of course Marell had come home after a few weeks. But now, whenever we went to see him, Sidnee wondered why she couldn't come with us.

We had begun to realize that whatever happened with Marell's case, he'd be gone for a very long time. So one day I sat Sidnee down and informed her that when people do wrong, there is a place where they go. Marell had done wrong, but he still loved her. Even when I explained Marell's situation this way, she didn't really understand where he was or why he couldn't come home. She just knew that Marell was her brother, that he loved her, and that she missed having him play with her and take her on bike rides and to the park.

On March 4th, Marell expressed that he was ready to see Sidnee. So one evening, I took her to the jail parking lot. We got out of the car, and when Marell saw us, he called us by three-way. He told Sidnee that he was watching her from a window. But she couldn't figure out where to look for him because she couldn't make out his face. That made Marell unhappy at first, then he became disgusted and upset. He felt bad when Sidnee asked him when he would be home again. It was a rough day for us all. There would be many more days when Sidnee visited him in that parking lot, and these visits got a little easier each time.

But overall, things got harder.

Mr. Stevenson had seen Marell only five times since he'd been in jail. I kept pushing for information and action with calls to the Public Defender Office, but all Mr. Stevenson could tell me was that he had not received any discovery and Marell's case had been continued until March 27th. I hated to have to tell my son about this delay. I could see that he was becoming more and more depressed.

Then, the following week, I got even worse news when I ran into Mr. Stevenson while I was dropping off clean underwear for Marell. Phillip had made a statement that would really hurt our case, Mr. Stevenson told me, accusing Marell of doing everything-negotiating with Mrs. Sawyer, creating the plan, pulling the trigger. Mr. Stevenson felt that given Marell's mood, he needed to settle down before he heard about Phillip's statement. So I waited before I became the messenger for bad news again.

Yes, Marell was angry. He'd been in jail for over a month, all the time believing his friend would remain true. But every time Marell had expressed to me that Phillip would not turn on him, I stressed, "You have no 'P's," using Marell's own way of calling a "partner," someone devoted to friendship. Marell was hurt badly by Phillip's betrayal. Just think: two lives ruined now, two lives that had spent the last ten years being friends, playing ball, and sharing time together. Look at them now, swept up in this storm.

Some days later, through one of Kesia's friends, we learned that Phillip had been approved for bond. This was hard to take. But he never was able to raise the money, so he stayed in jail until his sentencing. When Marell had been denied bond, I accepted the court's decision and tried to make him understand it too. I asked him, "Would you want bond for someone who killed your mother?" I wanted him to face reality. I had to talk tough to him. These were the times that he'd tear up and be my little boy again. This macho young man would break down only when I broke him down. "Ma, I never meant for this to happen," he'd cry. "We were only supposed to scare Mr. Sawyer. I never meant for it to go this far." Then I could see how sorry he was for his involvement. But these occasions were few and far between.

And then, for a while, I just shut down. I needed some thinking time. It was good that Marell had my Uncle Felton and Uncle Junior (as we always called my mother's brother Otis), as well as coaches, our minister, James, Kesia, and friends to hold down the visits for a few days. But I couldn't take much time off from the routine of visits and calls. However bad I was feeling, I knew my son was sinking into depression.

Even though Marell's case was stalled, time was flying by, and Easter came just as it did each year. For Sidnee, who was confused about what was happening with her big brother, we tried to make things as normal as possible. That meant buying a chick or baby duck, just as I had every Easter since Kesia and Marell were little. The week before Easter, I did the same and bought a baby duck that Sidnee named Honey, and Sid was having a fit for Marell to see it. Thinking that would uplift him, I bought an orange leash and trotted the duck right to the jail parking lot at the time of day Marell knew to look for us. He laughed and laughed and couldn't believe we had done that.

Later I became afraid that I might have embarrassed him. I had not even thought that this might have caused others in jail to pick on him. I was just trying to create normalcy for my son. But he later told me that a few inmates commented that his family was really special to think of him like that. And when James and I visited Marell that Easter Sunday, he was still laughing about Honey. Some months down the road, a man stopped me at a sports event and asked, "You are Boone's mother, right?" I told him I was, and he said he had been locked up for a while in the county jail with Marell. That man kind of chuckled when he said, "I was there when you brought the duck."

Our family also had another way of celebrating Easter Sunday. Everyone got a new outfit with matching colors to wear to church. Each year I'd pick a color for the dresses Kesia, Sidnee, and I wore, and the ties Marell and James wore with their suits. Even if James and Marell had different suits, their ties had to match. Kesia hated that we all had to have the same colors; she also hated her pretty little dresses that I had proudly made, even though Sidnee always loved hers. And later, I found out that Marell hated the suits. Even still, everyone smiled for the family pictures after church when we visited other family members' homes. To be sure all of us were included, I'd ask one of the family members to take the picture even though I considered myself a professional photographer, and I'd taken photography on as a part-time business. I'd insist on the right background, and everyone had to be in the right spot. James and I would stand together. Kesia and Marell would stand on each side of us, and I would hold Sidnee. Everyone had a place. I remember one picture in particular where our color was red. I had made myself a red polka dot dress. Luckily I had found a red polka dot dress for Sidnee, and I'd bought Kesia a red and white dress. James and Marell wore navy suits with red ties. I made copies of these pictures for all the family members, and of course, a picture went in the many photo books that I have accumulated over the years. I was very proud of those pictures.

But this Easter, there would be no family picture, no matching colors for us all, no new clothes for Marell.

Some weeks later, Marell started to attend church in jail. It made me happy that he'd go to services regularly; he needed all the strength that he could get from them. Within a few weeks, he announced on the phone that he was saved. He gave me no details about what went on at services or what he meant by being "saved." I'd heard that many guys in jail either join a gang or join a church. They join a church because they have done wrong and have the desire to be forgiven, to feel that everything is washed away and behind them. But I don't think you go into a church meeting and say to yourself, "I'm saved." I didn't think he'd had time for enough Bible study. I didn't believe that being saved was something magical that happened without a lot of consideration. I wanted to ask him, "How does this affect your soul?" "Do you really believe, or is this a babysitter for your comfort?" I dared not ask him the questions that were in my mind. I didn't want my doubts to interrupt his peace. If my son felt happy, I'd just accept what he told me.

Marell had seen a psychologist who worked with prisoners in the jail, and I was able to speak with him about the possibility of getting Marell medication for depression as well as Attention Deficit Disorder. When Marell had been in the second and third grades, I noticed he had trouble paying attention in class. Shortly after he began fourth grade, the school principal, a psychologist, and his teacher called me for a meeting. They felt Marell was not able to stay on task because of ADD. With medication, they thought Marell would settle down and concentrate.

But I thought the problem was that he was too immature for fourth grade and decided to have him put back into third. He was devastated by that move, so much so that many years later he told me how much he hated it. "I was melting down, Ma," he said. I was sad to hear him speak of his hurt and embarrassment after all that time. But I had to be honest with him even if he never agreed with the choice I'd made looking out for him. I did what I thought at that point was the right thing.

And now, there he was in jail where the GED program had finally started and Marell had been approved to participate. He liked leaving his cell each day to go to classes. Even still, he was depressed, and the psychologist observed it just like I did. Marell slacked up on calling every night. He'd wake up each morning feeling like he just couldn't take being in jail, couldn't take waiting a minute more for some news from the lawyer, or some announcement of a court date. So the psychologist arranged a prescription for Marell that helped him manage his studying as he worked through the GED program.

But when he took the test, he missed getting his high school equivalency diploma by one point. This was a setback, but we told him not to give up. He'd come so close. Mrs. Stevenson, who visited Marell in jail far more often than her husband, also encouraged him to try again. So he kept on preparing for the GED test and asking when it would be given.

Finally, one night he called to let us know that the test would be the following morning. And that morning, I went to my spot in the parking lot outside the jail, taking a chance that he or someone he knew would see me. I wanted to blow him a kiss for good luck. As I found out later, he was taking the test at exactly that moment. But it would be weeks before we learned the results.

At the same time Marell was studying for the GED exam, Kesia was at Duke University attending the federally funded LEAD (Leadership, Education and Development) program. It was for rising seniors who had been selected because they were leaders and had superior grades. Only a few qualified students were invited to attend.

Kesia had been a real leader at her school, starting groups dedicated to community work and establishing codes for dress and behavior. She had even run for student council president, and I'd helped her make her campaign signs. She didn't win, but we were proud that she was one of the two candidates for that position. Through everything, she earned excellent grades and loved to study, though being at school remained tense with people pointing her out as the sister of someone in jail for murder.

All this business with Marell had affected her. She struggled silently because my attention was focused on her brother. I was leaving her out and not even aware at times I was doing that. But while she was getting ready to leave home for Duke, I focused my attention on her, helping her prepare the pillows, sheets, towels, toiletries, and extra clothes she'd need while she was away. My grandmother, who always made sure that Marell, Kesia and Sidnee never went without, stepped up to help purchase these things. It was tough knowing that she'd be gone for six weeks and by herself for the first time, but I would be able to visit on weekends and restock anything that she needed. Kesia could hold her own and had a good head on her shoulders. This time away would refresh her. She was getting the break that she had earned and deserved, and I was glad for her.

Meanwhile, Marell waited several months for the result of that GED test, and finally he received a letter announcing that he had passed. When he called to tell us, I screamed for joy at the top of my lungs. GED or high school diploma, it did not matter. My first-born had graduated from high school. Marell and Phillip were the first to earn their GEDs in the Cumberland County Jail's on-site programs. The local newspaper even ran a notice about the success of this new program. But in jail, there were no celebrations for them, no cakes, no presents.

Despite everything that had happened to the Williams family, Marell had become a high school graduate, and Kesia was selected for a summer program at Duke. There were still things that I could be proud of, things that made me smile.

SIX

That Summer

But the shadow of worry darkened even the sunniest times. The day James and I took Kesia to Duke was also a visiting day at the jail. My stomach was turning because we were forced to miss our weekly visit with Marell. Trying to ease my mind, we stopped by the parking lot on our way out of town. We had told Marell what time to look out for us, and that was the next best thing to visiting him that day.

The next week he called saying that he had a sick feeling in his stomach. He never complained about such things, so this worried me. When I called the jail trying to get some information, I learned that the doctor was not scheduled to come for a few days.

Being powerless to take care of Marell that day reminded me of the first time I had felt that way. When he was just four months old, he'd been sick and crying for hours, non-stop. I was a first-time mother, very young and inexperienced. So I picked him up and walked to my mother's room, knocked on her door, and asked her what to do. What I really wanted was for her to get up and to take over for me. But she wouldn't. Through her closed door, she made a few suggestions and told me that he was my child and that I was the one to care for him.

Throughout the night I fussed at Marell, telling this little baby that he had to go to sleep because I had to get my rest. I had school the next morning. Finally, I took him to a pediatric emergency room where I cried so much that the doctor told me I would be no good to him if I didn't grow up and take responsibility.

Marell had infections in both ears, and the doctor prescribed antibiotics. Even after we got back home, I got no sleep. Still, the next morning, I took him to the babysitter, and then checked myself into high school. Being a young mother was rough, but I learned that I could take care of Marell, and I'm so thankful that my mother did not take over with him that night. She expected me to be responsible for my child, and that's how I began to learn to be a mother. And no matter the difficulties, motherhood became the most joyous part of life.

I'd have given anything now to be up all night taking care of Marell instead of lying awake worrying about him. I hadn't realized before what a comfort it was to me to be able to nurse him when he was sick. Now I couldn't take him to a doctor or an emergency room and had to rely on others who showed up only on scheduled days and didn't report anything to me.

Then there was a new, bigger worry. That summer, the whole jail was on lockdown for several days. Marell explained later that some guys had been arguing over the TV and as a punishment no inmate could have visitors or go to the canteen or watch TV or make phone calls. During lockdown, there wasn't even a way for Marell to look out the window when I came by each night.

When we finally had our next visit, was I happy to lay my eyes on him! He said that I always looked him up and down at a visit, and I did. I wanted to notice any changes on him, especially any kind of bruises or cuts, what with all the fights taking place in there.

Matter of fact, one day Marell called upset and said he needed to be moved. He said he could not get along with one of the inmates. That inmate was his co-defendant Phillip, the one who had turned on him and who was now housed in a cell next to Marell. Plus, in another cell close by, a racial incident was brewing.

Newspapers all across the country, even as far away as Los Angeles, covered the story of James N. Burmeister, a soldier in the 82nd Airborne at Ft. Bragg. He had just been arrested for killing two black people as part of his initiation into a white supremacist group. That act was supposed to earn him a spider web tattoo on his elbow, a symbol that he'd killed a non-white person. His arrest led to the discovery of a group of neo-Nazis in the army at Ft. Bragg, twenty-two of them in all, who were responsible for violence against blacks throughout the community. And now James N. Burmeister was another one of the inmates in that crowded Cumberland County Jail.

Marell wrote letters to the guards and the lieutenant expressing his concern. During one of my visits, I had the chance to speak to one of these lieutenants. I told him that I did not expect Marell to receive special treatment, but that I had real concerns for his safety. The next morning, when I took his clean underwear to the jail, I talked to another lieutenant. Soon after that, Marell notified me that he was moved to another cell, and he expressed his gratitude that I'd intervened. "I thank you for all you do for me, Ma." he said. But I let Marell know things would not always be fixed that easy.

Once things had settled down at the jail, I gave him some sad news that I'd been holding back. In fact, I dreaded seeing him the following week, but I had to tell him that Mike, one of his friends in the neighborhood, had been killed. Sadder still, the suspect in the shooting was also a friend. What were these young people thinking? Or should the question be, why were they not thinking at all?

I left my visit with Marell and went to give my condolences to Mike's family. His mother was sitting in a chair, her eyes bloodshot red from crying. I acknowledged her and greeted a room full of other neighbors and family members. Then I sat quietly a few minutes as people in the room chatted about how the killing occurred. I felt uneasy and sad. I couldn't imagine losing a child. My heart was aching for Mike's mother. As I got up to hug her, she mentioned that she had heard about Marell, and I told her how hard things had been. She whispered to me, "At least you can see your son. I will never see mine again. I will never see him again."

As bad as I felt about Marell being in jail and having to think about what he was dealing with daily, I knew there was something worse. Here was a mother with her only son gone forever. My son was alive.

Summer was our busiest time at the rec center what with twenty-five plus campers, sports and other side activities going on. I was still having moments when I'd run to the bathroom and cry. My supervisor, B. Louis Rogers (we called him "B."), was supportive and understanding. He had known my children since they were little and considered himself part of our family. Looking back, I wonder if he put more responsibilities on me that summer to distract my mind from Marell's situation. Being so busy was helpful, at times.

Marell was calling more regularly, and it was costing. During one call, he was arguing back and forth with another inmate. Fearing that a fight would break out, I fussed at him and told him to stop. But he said those guys were disrespecting me by being loud and cursing where I could hear them. Disrespecting me! Why was Marell worried about a little thing like those men cursing when *he* had not thought how he was disrespecting his family five months prior?

There were these two sides to Marell, and here was the side that cared about me and tried to protect me, even in little things. Once when he was about three years old, he saw that I was upset and sat beside me on the bed. He took two of his fingers and wiped my tears. Then he took two fingers from his other hand, put them up to his mouth, licked them, and used his wet fingers to wipe under my eyes and clear my remaining tears. With barely full sentences, Marell said, "I won't let anyone hurt you no more. I'll get them." He meant that and had tried to come to my defense many times when he felt things weren't right.

Even when he was just a baby, I would talk to him like he was an adult, and he would look in my eyes and listen attentively. My family often talked about our bond and suggested that I treated Marell different than my girls. Years later, Kesia and Sidnee would express their true feelings about the whirlpool of emotions that tossed us around after his arrest. They felt that by me loving Marell differently, I loved him more.

"No, no, not at all!" I'd always argue. I loved all my children equally. Without a doubt, all three of them were my world. But each one needed me in different ways. And yet, I can see how the girls felt that Marell got more of me than they did. With everything I had to do for him, especially during that summer of 1996, they came second to him, not in my love but in my thoughts and time and worry.

On July 18th, James and I had a meeting with the Stevensons that lasted almost three hours. Mrs. Stevenson told us that it was time to start contacting the rest of those people on the list we'd given them in February. These were the important people in Marell's life who could give information on his character. When we made up that list, we had hoped the Stevensons would have gotten right on it, that things would move boom, boom, boom. But now, months later, Mrs. Stevenson had interviewed only my grandmother and my Uncle Felton, Cheryl and her mother. My mother and brother were due to visit from Texas in a couple of days, and Mrs. Stevenson wanted to contact them as soon as they arrived.

The next day, on July 19th, Mrs. Stevenson called to say that the grand jury had convened on July 8th and had determined there was enough evidence to charge Marell. *On the 8th?* Why hadn't they given us this news at our meeting? Was it because they didn't want to tell us face to face? And by the time Mrs. Stevenson called us, she had already told Marell that he had been indicted. He was now officially charged with first-degree murder and conspiracy to commit murder.

Mrs. Stevenson worried how Marell was taking this news. He seemed to be handling it calmly, I told her. But me, that was a different story, even though James and I had thought we were prepared for what was coming. The words "indicted for first degree murder" slapped me in the face. Marell was getting tuned up to go to prison, maybe for the rest of his life, and all because of being *stupid*! Why? He was not a bad person. In fact, when we had that meeting with the attorney, the first thing he said was that Marell was concerned not about himself, but about how his situation was affecting his parents. How did my son, who could be thoughtful and kind, get himself into this mess?

Soon after the indictment, my family arrived from Texas, and my mother visited Marell by herself. She talked the Bible to him as she often did to her family, her students, or to anyone in reach to listen. Her conversation with Marell broke him down. He was full of emotions and cried on and off during their whole visit. He expressed his sorrow over all that had happened and how he had disappointed us. Part of my heart was relieved that he released feelings that had been bottled up. But another part hated to hear that because I knew our disappointment would keep him depressed.

Several days later there was more news to depress Marell. Mrs. Stevenson visited him in jail and explained what had turned up in discovery. The tests for gunshot residue on Marell's hands and clothes had turned up nothing. Same for tests for his fingerprints on the gun. Nothing. So there was no evidence against him beyond the statements-his, Phillip's, and Mrs. Sawyer's. The statements from Phillip and Mrs. Sawyer pinned everything on Marell and affected him so bad that he did not call for a couple of days.

By the weekend, my brother, Lamont, and I went to visit Marell. He seemed a little more upbeat and was very glad to see us. For a change, his face had a real smile with those dimples that I loved to see. But that smile did not last long because our conversation soon switched to the subject of the discovery.

"You could be looking at some serious time," Lamont said.

"Yeah, I know," Marell answered and stared into space. "Serious time" was bad, but there was the worse possibility, the death penalty.

People have asked me if fear about Marell's sentence hung over me every minute of every day. It may seem strange, but thinking about my son going off to prison for years, or for the rest of his life, was something I just didn't let myself do. As to the death penalty, I never allowed that thought to take hold. Never did I claim the idea that he would die for this crime. I had enough to put one foot in front of the other each day, to deal with the crisis of the day.

Like problems with Marell's laundry. It was part of my normal routine, until one night that summer when he called to let me know that he had not received the package I'd brought to the jail for him. Marell had never made comments about his laundry other than to thank me, but that night he let me know that he hadn't been given his laundry several times. Days might pass before staff would deliver it to him. I assured him that I would address this problem with the staff, and I did.

It was incidents like the one with the laundry that made me leery about leaving for my usual summer trip to visit family in Texas. I feared no one would take care of Marell the way I did. I drilled James about exactly what his responsibilities would be. I talked to him about the schedule of visits and how to get clean underwear to our son. I repeatedly called Mrs. Stevenson to find out just where we were with the case or any court dates. I wanted to make sure that nothing crucial would go on while I was away. She assured me that there would be no changes or court dates before I returned. And while I was away, every time I talked to James I asked if he had heard anything from Marell.

By the summer of 1996, I had learned a lot about how to be the mother of a young man in jail. When I wanted him moved to another cell for his safety or when I wanted to talk to someone when he was sick or when I wanted to check on his laundry or the money that had been deposited to his account, I couldn't just pick up the phone, call the jail, and talk to a lieutenant or doctor or nurse or accountant. I had to respect the chain of command, so I was careful about who I talked to, and how. I wouldn't want to go over someone's head or get information from a sympathetic staff member and wind up making things worse for my son. I maneuvered with my tone whenever I spoke to anyone. But whenever I had the opportunity, I let staff know my ears were open wide. I learned that you had to make people aware who you are, that you're there, and that you care.

And when there was so much I couldn't control, dealing with the ordinary problem of the day-like laundry-was a way I could control *something*.

SEVEN

That Fall, the Holidays, and Another Year Begins

Every now and then a problem that was not an ordinary one jolted our lives, like the one at the end of the summer, when Marell was offered a plea. If he took it, he'd have a hearing in October. But he was adamant that he would not accept it because it carried a twenty-five-year sentence. He had come under the influence of those jailhouse lawyers who counseled that a trial by jury would find him not guilty.

"You're being set up. You keep calling their bluff," they told him.

So Marell kept saying to me, "I'm going to trial; they don't have no evidence."

And I kept telling him, "You have no idea what a jury will do. There might be just one person who sways the others to find you guilty." I expressed to Marell that I was disappointed and disgusted that he wouldn't accept the plea. Still, he rejected it.

About this time, Marell explained during one of our visits that a trustee had passed on a threat from another prisoner. A trustee is a prisoner who earns his position by supposedly being trustworthy and who travels though each unit of the jail selling canteen items. But this particular trustee also carried gossip and threats back and forth. Marell became agitated, convinced that the prisoner would take action. I responded lightly about this because I wanted my son to remain composed and responsible. But he was emotional when he asked that I call Mr. Stevenson at home to inform him of the threat.

Then there was another jolt that put Marell in a depressive state. He got word from a mutual friend that Phillip had agreed to a plea of ten to fifteen years. Marell thought about the plea that he had turned down. Why had Phillip received an offer of shorter time?

A few days later, the jolts continued. Mr. Stevenson decided to leave the Public Defender Office for private practice. What would this mean to our son? Would the next PD have the same passion to defend Marell? Could the court allow Mr. Stevenson to continue as Marell's lawyer, even when he'd left the PD Office? We hated to think how long it would be before a new attorney was appointed and then how much longer it would take to catch him up on Marell's case.

Mrs. Stevenson continued to work on it and was as helpful as she could be. She even inquired if her husband might be able to continue as Marell's defense attorney. On October 15th, James and I wrote to the judge who was in charge of appointing that person: "As parents we have pondered for many days as to whether it would be appropriate to write this letter." We explained Marell's situation and our concern that Mr. Stevenson was leaving the Public Defender Office. "It is not our desire to condone or excuse Marell's actions," we wrote, "yet to focus on support and fairness to him." We knew that the court would decide who Marell's attorney would be. If it was not to be Mr. Stevenson, we requested that Mr. Alfred Porter be appointed. Then we concluded the letter: "Our hearts ache and our thoughts are twisted as we think of Marell's future. Hence, through trust in God, we trust that any decision made will be just. We appreciate your time and dedicated concern in this matter. May God bless you!"

While Marell was in jail and during the years after that, I tried to help him by writing many letters to a judge or lawyer or staff member. I'd also leave phone messages for these people, when that was possible. Yet I realized they had many cases to consider, while I had only one son. I always made the effort for Marell even though I knew that most likely, I wouldn't get a response.

So I didn't take it personally when the judge didn't answer our letter, or when Mr. Stevenson was not allowed to continue as Marell's attorney, or when Mr. Porter was not appointed. Finally, someone was appointed, but I don't remember his name because we met him only once. Then Mr. Copeland, another attorney, came on the scene. I can't remember his first name because we saw him face-to-face no more than twice. Although we did a lot of talking on the phone, he didn't stick with the case either. But he did bring a second plea bargain to Marell, and Marell turned that one down too. Then, during a phone conversation, Mr. Copeland told me that Mr. Timothy Drake would be appointed, and Mr. Drake stuck with the case until Marell was sentenced.

When Marell was arrested, I started a journal as a way to keep meetings and people straight in my mind, but by the time Mr. Drake took over in the spring of 1997, I had not written in the journal for several months. It had become too much for me, just one more job every day. So I have no notes about details of the pleas or Marell's statement when I saw it for the first time. My memory is blurry because I blocked a lot of what was happening. I was burned out and had simply shut down inside.

The normal parts of my life were no longer normal. Things that I had looked forward to and celebrated in the past were now all considered in reference to Marell in jail. We had made the best of our first Easter without him at home. Then there were more firsts: in May, Sidnee's birthday on the 7th, followed by Mother's Day-the most important day of the year for me ever since I gave birth to my children-and then James's birthday on the 15th. The first this, the first that. Our first 4th of July party, my birthday in October, then Thanksgiving and Kesia's birthday on December 18th.

I realize now that I only went through the motions of celebrating. We did the things that normal families were doing. It was a struggle, but we didn't skip a beat. We had to do that, for the girls. But my heart wasn't in it like before.

And then came the first Christmas.

I'd always done Christmas up big. I'd bake oatmeal, chocolate chip, and sugar cookies as well as sweet potato, coconut (James's favorite), and pecan pies. I'd make decorations, and we'd decorate our tree as a family. I'd sew stockings and hang them from a shelf. The children were sometimes more excited by a stocking filled with treats and goodies than they were by the gifts wrapped in pretty paper.

But that Christmas of 1996, I did not get involved in decorating. If it had been up to me, I wouldn't have put anything up. I told James that I just couldn't do what I'd done before. So he went out and bought the tree and decorated it with the girls while I sat in my bedroom feeling numb.

On Christmas day, we did give each other gifts as usual, and I wanted to cook a turkey as well as some of the favorite foods that those dear to me would expect to taste. I recalled how Marell would enjoy certain dishes that I'd cooked and wished he could be at the dining room table with us. James led the grace, and even though he mentioned Marell's absence, to have other members of my family enjoy that Christmas meal brought me a feeling of quiet peace and fulfillment. I could still feel joy when I cooked for James and the girls, my grandmother, my aunt, uncle, and cousins.

But on January 14th, Marell's first birthday behind bars hit me hard. Birthdays were big in the Williams household. Each person picked how to celebrate. As Marell and Kesia grew older, they would want to spend their big day with friends or maybe have a family night out. Marell's 20th birthday would be so different, and not just because he was leaving his teen years behind. There would be no homemade German chocolate cake waiting on the table for him. There would be no birthday sign over the living room sofa.

Despite the sadness that never completely left us, I had found a way to bring joy to my family with a Christmas meal, so I came up with the best way for us to celebrate Marell's birthday. I made the birthday sign and bought the balloons, and by the time James got home from work that afternoon, I was ready to go with him to the jail parking lot.

On schedule, Marell was looking from the window when we got out of our car. I held up the sign and Sidnee held the balloons. A breeze shifted the balloons around and around, and we had to keeping turning so Marell could see them from his angle. When our call went through on the three-way phone hook-up, we began to sing "Happy Birthday."

"Son, your mom and her wild ideas," James said. He had been afraid our display would not be a good idea, that it might embarrass Marell. But we recalled that when we brought Honey the duck to the parking lot on Easter, some of the other inmates thought Marell was lucky to have a family that cared so much about him.

"Ma, you are too much," Marell laughed.

EIGHT
Partings

I began to see that every sadness was uplifted by some happy event, even as every happy time was tinged with a little sadness.

We had staggered into the new year. Cases were backlogged in the courts, especially murder cases. We were stuck in a rut. I kept up the weekly visits with Marell. Each evening, I'd be in the parking lot where he knew to look for me through the window of his cell. Each week, I collected his laundry, washed it, and returned it on schedule. I kept up my calls to the attorney and to the prison staff when something was off. We continued to deposit money in Marell's account and accept as many collect calls as he could make and we could afford. It seemed like I was having the same bad dream over and over and that it would never stop. I realized it would be a long time before Marell got out of that overcrowded, dangerous jail.

But like I said, sometimes I'd wake up and sunshine broke through the clouds.

Kesia was preparing to graduate from high school. All the while Marell had been in jail, she stayed independent, keeping up her grades and extra curricular activities. She'd submitted her applications to favored universities, and she'd been accepted into several. But the University of North Carolina at Chapel Hill was pretty much all she ever talked about. And were we proud when that acceptance letter arrived in the mail! Then her scholarships and funding put the period at the end of the sentence. Still, I was nervous about many things, including how we would budget for any cost that was not covered.

When my grandmother took ill and became more feeble, I prayed that she would be able to go to Kesia's graduation. Grandma loved all my children and did whatever she could for them, but Kesia had wrapped Grandma right around her little finger. Grandma catered to her and fixed all her favorite foods. Kesia cuddled up in her bed any time she wanted to. So Grandma was looking forward to seeing her walk across the stage, and I'm so grateful that she was able to be there with me and James and Sidnee.

Kesia's graduation was a happy day in June, even though Marell expressed his sadness that he could not be there. I assured him I'd take plenty of pictures, and I did. I snapped James looking proud and nervous, just like I was. We shared tears and smiles throughout the ceremony. Our daughter had done something that made us so proud. She had succeeded and followed through with her potential, where Marell had not.

Thinking back to that summer, I see how my emotions were in a twister that could lift me from side to side and land me no telling where or in what state. Just like a twister, my feelings twirled me around and around because people I loved were leaving.

My Grandma, my *rock*, had tried to prepare me when she only had a short time left on this earth. She always knew the things that were heavy on my heart. When I talked to her, I'd get my bearings. She kept me on the right path and gave me hope. The night before she closed her eyes for the last time was no different. In those quivering moments, some of the few words she spoke were about Marell: "I know that boy. He didn't shoot that man. That don't make no sense what that woman did."

I had expressed to Grandma that I wanted to write a book about Marell, and from her deathbed, she encouraged me to do it. "The one thing I want you to do is to finish writing your book," she said. That night she also told me not to worry about paying Kesia's college expenses, regardless of whether she got all the scholarships she'd applied for. Grandma had been careful keeping her accounts, so I knew what she meant. She assured me that everything would work out. And everything did.

Once again Major Whirley showed our family kindness and consideration. It was unusual for someone in jail to be allowed to attend a funeral for anyone besides an immediate family member-a father, mother, or sibling. But Major Whirley allowed Marell to attend Grandmother's funeral. My Uncle Junior paid the fee to cover the expenses for guards to accompany him, and I bought Marell a suit so that he wouldn't have to wear his prison clothes.

Years before, I had been to another funeral where inmates were in attendance. When I was a child, my great-aunt died. Both her sons were in jail at the time, and they came to her service with their hands shackled behind them. Their feet were shackled too, and even before I saw them, I heard them coming, their shackles clang, clang, clanging on the steps into the funeral home. I'll never forget watching one of my cousins lean over to kiss my great-aunt in her casket. I'd never seen anyone kiss a dead person before. Other than that, my cousins weren't allowed to get closer than two feet from any of us. The guards were white and had such a superior expression on their faces.

But Grandmother's funeral was different. In our grief, we were comforted to have our son with us, and so happy at the way Marell's two guards handled everything. I don't remember their names, but I do recall that one was black, the other white. I can see that man's face in my memory today, maybe because his was the only white face surrounded by all the black faces in my grandmother's country church. When we sang "Precious Lord," he told me that hymn was sung at his grandmother's church, too.

Though it was horrible to see Marell's legs chained together, the chains ran under his pant legs through his shirt and to his arms. His hands were cuffed together in the front, not in back, so I could hold them throughout the whole service. Family members were allowed to say goodbye to Marell at the sheriff's car and speak to him and hug him. The guards even stepped aside so that we could have a picture with just the family in it. How kind of them to let us take that picture! One of them was so struck by our sadness that tears rolled down his cheeks. These men who had seen so much, who could have been so hardened, were very tender that day. I would surely like to thank them again-as I thanked Major Whirley many times-for being so kind.

At the end of August, we brought our daughter to Chapel Hill to begin her freshman year in college. She showed little emotion in the car and while we were helping set things up in her dorm room. We met her roommate, who seemed very nice, but I wished her parents had been there, too. You can tell so much more about a person if you meet some of their family.

I didn't want to leave Kesia that day. Any parent who's moved a child into her college dorm room knows how I was feeling. You're pleased for her, you wouldn't want her to be living at home when she has so many opportunities ahead. Yet you are sad that a part of your life with her is over.

Kesia stayed calm, but of course I was emotional and crying. Finally James stepped in and said, "Now look Rosalind, it's time for us to go."

And six weeks later, the day came for Marell to go.

Phillip had accepted his plea and gone to prison, Mrs. Sawyer had accepted her plea, but Marell had rejected two pleas. Then he was offered a third plea bargain, and he accepted. We tried to talk about it, but he wouldn't discuss it with us. He was tired of the back and forth. He wanted one phase to be over and the next one to start. And James and I refrained from discussing it with each other. Like Marell, I just wanted the uncertainty to be over.

When the final court date was appointed, even though we'd waited so long, there was no way to prepare for it. On the morning of October 9, 1997, we were quiet. Perhaps we should have been sitting at our dining room table, eating breakfast, drinking coffee, and discussing our son's future. Instead, James and I were silently getting dressed and passing each other in the bedroom as we prepared to go to court.

We had gotten up in plenty of time, still we were running late when we closed the front door. Maybe I had taken too much time to pray. I prayed every chance I could, asking for strength, asking for guidance, and asking any decision to be kind, compassionate and forgiving to my son, just as God forgave us.

By the time we got to the courthouse, the parking lot was full and no parking space was in sight. I remember thinking, why wasn't there a closer parking space? We were Marell's parents! Didn't folks know what we were going through? My thoughts were selfish, I realize that now, but then all I could feel was fear about what we faced.

Once in the courtroom, the same courtroom where Marell had been arraigned twenty months before, we got settled in our seats next to other family and friends. I looked towards the inmate box for Marell, but the jailers had not brought him in yet. The Honorable Lee Cramer heard a couple of cases before Marell arrived. When he did, he looked around the courtroom for us until we made eye contact. That was some solace for him, seeing us there. But when I saw him like that, my skin cringed. I began to shake. Tears would not stop running down my face. James took a hold of my shoulders and squeezed them tight.

In a matter of minutes, we heard Judge Cramer call out: "Marell La-Trek Williams." The judge sounded distant. He was just reading words when he asked his questions, as if he had no care at all about who Marell was as a person. Could Marell hear the charges read? Had anyone threatened him into taking a plea? Was he a citizen of the United States? Was he under the influence of drugs or alcohol? Did he understand by taking this plea he was giving up the right to plead not guilty? After Marell answered all the questions, the judge declared:

> These are the terms of your plea. Upon acceptance of your plea to the charge of second-degree murder, the Court will impose a minimum 196-month, maximum 245-month sentence; to the charge of conspiracy to commit murder, the court will impose a concurrent 96-month minimum, 122-month maximum sentence.

Then Mr. Drake spoke for Marell:

> Your honor, he has specifically requested that I express his deepest regrets to the victim's family and to all others affected by this incident as well as his own regrets at having hurt his family and them having

go through this. It is . . . his intent to make the very best of a bad situation at the time that he is imprisoned.

The procedure was short. My son's sentencing was over.

But Mr. Drake had a final request for the court. He pointed to James, my mother, and me and asked the judge to allow Marell to have a few minutes with us before he was taken away. Judge Cramer agreed, and Marell was led into a hall where a sheriff kept a close eye on us as we huddled together and hugged him, though he couldn't hug back because his hands were shackled behind his back. There was no privacy. Marell was trying to hold back his tears, but they started rolling down his face. We were all crying.

Too soon, the sheriff led Marell away to jail.

"Did you do this?" I had asked Marell when the police brought him home right after he was arrested.

"No ma'am," he answered. I believed him and stood strong on this and what my grandmother said on her deathbed, that Marell was innocent.

You may think that I was stupid and naïve, but the words "my son committed murder" never came out of my mouth. I simply didn't believe he had pulled the trigger.

Even still, the mother in me justified that Marell was there. But what could have possibly explained how he'd been party to a man's murder? Why had he? How could he?

I frequently asked him what really happened that night, but I had to pick my time for this question when we were by ourselves and Marell seemed upbeat. My mind burst to know and stretched to crazy motives. Had it been gang related? I had no evidence of that. I was pulling at straws to understand what had brought Marell to this point. I even asked if there been anything sexual between him and Mrs. Sawyer. Did that question ever make Marell mad! And really, how did I dare ask that?

And when I asked the most important question, about the moment of the shooting, he responded that everything went blank.

I can never deny that my son had been involved with something very bad. I had never claimed that he should not go to jail. I had preached to my children all their lives that their actions had consequences, and rewards or punishments would follow.

Rewards or punishments. Rewards or punishments. All the love I had for Marell couldn't wash away the fact that he would be in prison for a long time.

"God is not going to put more on you than you can bear," I would tell him: "Pray and speak the words out loud." If I said that once, I said that hundreds of times.

Even though I tried to see God's hand directing our lives, I couldn't help feeling the unfairness of it all. Three people had been arrested for Mr. Sawyer's death, but Marell was sentenced for a lot longer than Phillip, whose sentence was for ten to thirteen years. And Mrs. Sawyer, the woman who'd snared two young men into ruining their lives, she was sentenced to five to seven years, while Marell could be in prison for over twenty. He might be forty when he got out with the best years of his life behind him. If he'd gone into the navy, he could have retired by that time.

So I asked myself: Had I encouraged him to take his plea just because I was worn out waiting for it? This is one of the questions that I will never have answered.

My concentration turned to how I was going to cope with Marell being in prison. I tried to remain positive; he could get college courses or learn a trade. Still my heart hurt because he would be far away from us. There would be no more instant visits to the parking lot. What I had seen on TV about prison told me there would be fighting, drugs, and gangs. The thought of him being with people who were violent and without caring hearts frightened me. In my little world, I believed that Marell was somewhat better than they were. I had not processed it before, but now it was *real* that my young son was to be amongst grown men *in prison*. I feared that he would not be ready for this type of life.

And so I prayed, "Lord, help me to be there whenever I can. Help him to never, ever forget that he has a family that cares and will be there always for him."

II

Visiting the Prisons
October 10, 1997, to May 28, 2012

NINE
Transition

On October 10, 1997, the day before my birthday, Marell was shipped out of Cumberland County Jail in the middle of the night. I heard about this in a call from an inmate; I don't remember his name. That day I learned prisoners were moved from one place to another often in the middle of the night, with no warning, not knowing where they were going. I suppose this was a secure means of transporting prisoners rather than having them and their loved ones know when and where they'd be on the road. It was also one of the many ways that we saw how little control we had over Marell's life. But as I also learned that day, Marell would always try to ask another prisoner to call to let us know that he was being moved, even if he didn't know where he was going.

That evening, Marell called us himself from Polk Correctional Center, which was located on Old Blue Ridge Road in Raleigh. He gave us the visiting schedule and the directions to get there, but he sounded so distant. He was sorry that he was missing my birthday and hated Polk already. He'd gotten used to things in Cumberland County Jail, where he knew the ropes and was somebody. Now he was the low man on the totem pole in a place that was much stricter. I reminded him that this was just the beginning, and he needed to make the best of the situation. That was advice I needed to take myself, because I just wanted to shut everyone and everything out.

Sunday, October 12th, the day of our first visit, came quick. I hated to miss church, yet in order to be at Polk on time, James, Sidnee, and I needed to get on the road. Marell expected us early and would be ready. This would be just the second time in twenty months that Sidnee would see her brother face to face. She'd seen him at my grandmother's wake, but she'd never come with us to visit him in the jail, and she couldn't really see him when we'd wave at each other from the parking lot. Having the two of them together would be a joy to my heart. Plus, I would be putting my arms around my son. In my mind, I imagined holding him during the whole visit.

The drive took just an hour. Polk was an initial processing place for male offenders between the ages of nineteen and twenty-one. Several small buildings were surrounded by double fences with barbed wire at the top. Correctional officers—we learned to call them the "COs"—sat in a security tower and could see visitors as they approached. During that first visit to Polk, only a few people were in line waiting to see prisoners, which was good for us because the length of our visit would depend on the number of visitors that day. The fewer the visitors, the longer we'd have. And checking in was pretty simple. James and I showed our IDs and Sidnee's birth certificate.

Once I got inside, I could see just how run down the place was. It had been built way back in 1920 on the grounds of a World War I United States Army tank base. Back then, inmates farmed the land. While Marell was there, most of the 381 inmates slept in crowded dormitories with double bunks. The bathrooms and showers were right in front of the dormitories. Because Polk was an intake facility, inmates were screened and tested as soon as they got there. Those with less than a sixth-grade education had to take classes. Some of them went to work on a GED. Others were assigned to cleaning or work in the canteen or some other job. But the place was overall unfit for humans to live in and was soon to be replaced with a new facility in Durham. Thankfully, Marell would not be at Polk very long.

An officer led us to an area that seemed to be a small cafeteria; across the room was the actual cooking area. Pots and pans hung down from a rack that was attached to the ceiling; the stoves were visible too. We sat around a table on round stools that were small and uncomfortable, as if no one expected us to be sitting on them for very long. Even still, James managed to have Sidnee sit on his lap.

In a few minutes, we heard a voice call over the intercom, "Marell Williams." In another five minutes, I spotted him coming in a door to the right. He had the biggest smile on his face. I stood up, stepped towards him, and grabbed that child so tight. This was our first real hug since the day he was arrested. Yes, I'd hugged him at Grandma's funeral and in the hall right after his sentencing, but he couldn't hug back because his hands were chained together. Who was timing that hug? Not me. Bad as it was that he was in prison, at least now I could hug him at each and every visit.

As we walked back to the table, Sidnee ran to Marell. Joy ran through my body at the sight I had waited so long to see-the embrace of my little girl and my son. It was just a hugging good time with us all.

But not for long. A guard quickly guided Marell to sit on the opposite side of a table from us. That was okay, though, because I could still touch him. I grabbed his hand and held it throughout the entire visit. The hour went fast.

Was this what I had to look forward to for years to come? It wasn't fair that our time was so short, I thought. I needed more time. James pulled me toward the door while Sidnee and I both cried. After we buckled her up in the car, she asked us, "Why does Marell have to stay there?" I didn't answer. Sidnee was only six years old, but she asked the question I asked myself so many times. Why?

And then a conversation with my other daughter forced me down some pathways of deep soul searching. Marell had arrived at Polk around the time of Kesia's fall break, when she and I were running errands together. She had tried several times to explain how different I seemed to treat her in comparison to Marell. Yet that day, sitting so close to each other in my car where there was no escape, her words hit my heart. I reacted, snappy, and she came back full force. She went on about the way I always visited Marell's classroom for conferences but talked with her teachers only briefly.

"Mama," she said, "You never came to my room during parent teacher conferences." Believe it or not, that was the same thing she'd said to me on the first day Marell went to jail. I tried once more to explain my reasoning. Her teachers had always stopped me in the hall and bragged about how excellent her grades were. I juggled my words to justify why I felt Marell needed more guidance and attention than she did. Our conversation went on and on, and we never came to a happy medium.

My heart was too heavy to make up or make her understand that my children were my world, words she had heard from me many times before. I had not ignored the girls on purpose. I only tried to do what I thought was best.

For the first time, though, she made me ask myself: Was I really guilty of unfair treatment that I had never before owned up to? Her words impacted me so hard that I asked myself: "Rosalind, did you really do this?"

Marell had certain days he was allowed to call, and I cherished every one. But calls cost more from prison than they had from jail, so we had to stick with only two a week, on Wednesday and Sunday. Believe it not, there are some prisoners whose families just won't accept collect calls because they don't have the money. But Marell knew that if he couldn't call us, my parents, sisters, and my aunt Rutha Mae would always accept his calls. He knew he had certain people he could count on.

And when we spoke to him, he talked strong, like everything was under control. But life was a lot rougher at Polk than it had been at the county jail, which was smaller and tighter. Guards could get to inmates faster if they started fighting. At the jail, there was no yard for exercise where a prisoner could use a shank before a guard could stop him. There were no stairwells out of the guards' sight where one prisoner could jump another. I feared getting a call that Marell's body had been found at the bottom of those stairs.

Marell told us that prisoners grouped together. They were constantly involved in territorial fights, and Marell saw one coming between a Fayetteville and a Charlotte gang. He wasn't at Polk more than six weeks before he got into a fight. Someone got into his space, and he felt he had to prove himself. He apologized to us for getting into trouble, but still he said to me, "You got to fight, Ma. I got to let them know I'm no punk."

I didn't want him to fight, but I knew what he said was true. Turning the other cheek would be seen as weakness. All I could do was to pray every night that God would bring him back to me in his good health and with a sane mind. I wanted him to *survive*, yes, but my greatest desire was that he be faithful to God and do right. I wanted him to stand on the foundations that he was raised with. I wanted these to direct and guide him through any storm. Our family's beliefs were the pillars that could hold him up. Yet I asked myself, could he survive *and* be true to those beliefs?

Just two months into his sentence, he received his first two offenses for fighting and disobeying direct orders to stop. According to prison procedure, he was charged. Then prison officials reviewed the circumstances of the fight. Then came a letter outlining the offense and announcing when and for how long he'd have to spend time in solitary confinement as his punishment. At Polk, "lockup" or "the hole," as prisoners call it, was in a separate segregation unit that only had eighteen cells, so prisoners had to be scheduled for it in advance. Marell was to start his thirty-day lockup on the 29th of December.

Right before Christmas on December 21st, the girls and I had one more visit with him. My mother, who had traveled up from Texas, came too, and we had a happy time, even though we knew Marell would be going into solitary the following week. We forced ourselves not to think about that.

And not only did we get a visit, we were allowed to bring Marell a box of snacks and home-cooked food as special Christmas treats. Each item had to be clear wrapped or in plastic bags. My brother-in-law worked at a sandwich shop and made Marell special sandwiches filled with meat of every kind. Also, I stuffed into a box Marell's favorite snacks, like beef jerky, cashews, sunflower seeds, gummy bears, and, of course, Snickers. It seemed like a lot, yet I knew he'd go through it in a matter of days.

When we arrived for the visit, we had to give all the gifts of food to the COs who divided and smashed the sandwiches and snacks to detect anything odd or illegal within them. I felt that the prisoners were being belittled by getting this messy food, and I couldn't understand how they would want those items after they'd been pulled apart. But they did, because it was a taste of home. This food would be Marell's only Christmas gift besides the tennis shoes that I ordered for him.

But Christmas just wasn't exciting to me any more, and like the year before, James took over while I sat around moping. He decorated the Christmas tree, tables, and windows for the girls' sake, especially for young Sidnee. My Christmas spirit was gone.

Marell went to lockup on December 29th. My heart hurt every time I thought of him being completely isolated in a separate building on the Polk grounds. I thought about what it would be like for me to be in a confined area, alone, with no one to talk to. There would be no communication with other prisoners, no phone calls or visits from us, or anyone. For just one hour each day, he would be taken out of his cell for exercise and fresh air.

I feared for how Marell would handle this. I imagined him in a room down in a dungeon, in a hole. From TV, I learned about the worst of these places, like the segregation unit on Rikers Island. Being in solitary can scramble a man's brains, especially a young man's brain if it is not fully formed. Men start hallucinating and talking to themselves. Sometimes guards make the situation even worse by withholding food or knocking it off the trays. Angry inmates sometimes act out by spreading urine or feces on the walls, so their cells become filthy and full of bacteria.

But it wasn't that bad at Polk. There were many prisoners walking around the segregation unit, some of them delivering food to the men in their cells. At least Marell had some human contact, though I was afraid that by talking to anyone he'd be breaking the rules and get into more trouble. Still, I was relieved, because I know people can lose their minds in a very short time when they're in isolation.

And another good thing: he was able to write and receive as many letters as possible, so I wrote a letter every few days. I prayed my letters would bring him life.

TEN

Prison for Real

On the night of January 15, 1998, I got two surprises. The first was a call from Marell telling me he had been moved that morning to a place called the Foothills Correctional Institute in Morganton, North Carolina. The second surprise was to learn that he would no longer be in lock-up there. I did not question the why or ask what had changed.

Marell let me know that visitation would be on Saturdays. He was already very vocal about not liking the place, and he expressed the same thing in a couple of letters before we actually had the opportunity to visit. "Everyone is in for a long time," he wrote, "they just don't care." Prisoners did not fight with their hands. They fought with knives, shanks, and objects that caused real harm. Marell's letters led me to think that he had already observed or even experienced some bad action. Still, he tried not to portray fear and reminded me that I hadn't raised a "punk." "This is the roughest place my long journey is going to take." He really didn't have a clue what was coming.

Marell always ended his letters with thankfulness and love to the family. In one letter, he added a footnote to request that I listen to "Mama" by Boyz to Men. In this song, a man thanks his mother for loving him even when he was bad because her love gave him the strength to do right. That song gave me hope that Marell would stay the course. But it was the chorus that reached deep into my heart, and I can still hear Marell singing the words, "Lovin' you is like food to my soul."

Because Marell wanted "Mama" to be our theme song for 1998, I felt sure my prayers were being answered. He will be okay, I told myself. He will be okay.

According to the directions I found, it would take four hours and ten minutes to drive to Foothills, which was in the western part of North

Carolina, outside of Morganton. Well, that distance shook me. I wasn't a long-distance driver. I could barely drive two-and-a-half to three hours without my eyelids getting heavy. James would be going on the initial visit, but what about the rest? There would have to be some praying going on when I was driving by myself.

When I wanted to see Marell on prison visiting days, I always had to call a special officer in advance. That hadn't been necessary in jail. It had been so much easier because we could just show up at the appointed time and place. But at Foothills, there was a limit to the number of visitors on any given day, and after our first visit, I learned to call on Monday to be sure I would get my visit on Saturday.

During my first call, the officer explained some rules and reminded us to bring our IDs. He also warned us to get there early to be sure we got checked in on time. And he made the point that we always had to identify Marell by his prison number: 0588737. When we wanted to visit or send a letter or a money order, we had to use his number and only his number. Once when I forgot and addressed a letter with only Marell's name, it was returned. Even though the officer told us up front that my son's name was no longer important, the prison staff called him either by his nickname, Boone, or just Williams.

The closer it got to that first Saturday visit, the more nervous I became. Marell was on edge, too, and called the night before to be assured we were coming. The morning of the visit, I was what I'd call "crazy nervous." I had to select the right things to wear according to rules for visitors: nothing too tight, no pants cut too low that let skin or underwear show-not that I ever wore anything like that-but in the warmer weather I might like to wear open sandals or a sleeveless top, and they were also forbidden. I wanted my hair to look good. It was important that everything was right. I wanted to make Marell happy, and there were so few ways that I could do that. And everything had to be right in the house before we left. Was the door locked? Was the cooler in the car with our snacks and drinks for the road?

By the time we left at about 8:30, my mood even made my husband nervous. He led the prayer in the car for travel safety. And was it a long drive! It seemed like the longest four hours I had ever lived. Thankfully, Sidnee slept almost the whole trip except for when we stopped for a quick lunch.

As the altitude changed when we approached the mountain areas of Morganton, my ears began to slightly pop, and I saw exactly how "Foothills Correctional Institute" got its name. It's at the foothills of the Blue Ridge Mountains. The Catawba River, the Linville Gorge, and the Pisgah National Forest are all right nearby, but I couldn't focus on the beauty of fall-colored trees along the highway. Other people might visit Morganton for vacation or to see these beautiful places, but not us. We didn't notice any of it because as soon as we got to the town, we made a left turn and went down a long road with fewer and fewer houses on it.

Then we saw the brick buildings. They sat on some beautiful property with a clear view of the mountains behind them. The place had opened just four years earlier, so it was newer and cleaner than Polk, surely better in those ways. But Polk and Foothills were still the same and would remain the same: prison.

The parking lot was a distance from the prison itself. James, Sidnee, and I entered the long line of visitors around quarter 'til 2:00. I looked at all those people that were ahead of us and thought, "They're in the same boat as we are. We're all here to see our loved ones." But these visitors already knew the ropes, and in the future, we made a point of being there around 1:15 because it was past 2:00 by the time we got processed through and that cut time from our visit.

When the line started moving, we were directed to drop our IDs in a slot that led to officers behind a thick window. Next we passed through a weapon check device like you've seen at an airport. The COs checked our pockets and clothes. I knew no purses were allowed, so I had not brought one. In the future, when I'd drive up by myself, I carried only a small wallet that I could lock in the car.

After we passed inspection, we moved to another building that housed the visitation room. It was big room with square tables, and I was grateful that the chairs were more comfortable than they'd been at Polk. We heard Marell's name called, but it was a while before we actually saw him. Before entering this visiting area, he had to enter a room where he and other inmates stripped naked and bent over in front of guards who checked even between their butt cracks for any kind of weapons or contraband. This process was repeated after our visits so the guards could be sure inmates weren't bringing back into prison anything they shouldn't have. I hate to remember this detail of our visits. It demeaned Marell and the other prisoners to have to expose themselves. And these checks also took time away from our visits.

Finally, from where we were seated, we could see Marell approaching through a long hall. A few minutes later, he passed through a door leading into the room where we sat.

The first thing I noticed about him that day was his hair. It was longer than ever with little tweaks sticking up like he'd taken bits of hair and twisted them into half braids. I hated those little braids and wished he'd give in to a nice haircut. When I was teaching, I always counseled young men about their hair. I'd tell them that if they wanted to impress and get a good job, they needed to look clean-cut. I thought Marell would be treated better without those braids even in prison. Looking good and having a good attitude would make the staff think better of him and take better care of him.

Braids or not, I stood up and embraced him. Then Marell hugged Sidnee before he reached for his Dad. We had so much to catch up on. And did I have questions for him about the food and his sleeping space! But he never did elaborate on these things at Foothills or in any of the places where he was in prison. Because he asked me to mail him photographs of the family and those *Jet* magazine pictures of girls from the back of his bedroom door, I do know what he put up on the walls in his cells.

During that first visit at Foothills, he did tell us about what I really wanted to know-those fights he'd written about in letters. He filled us in on the many people that he knew from Fayetteville. Even though they usually tried to look out for one another, I begged him to stay away from cliques that would be nothing but trouble.

But he boasted that he had influence around there already, and we never discussed how that came about. He never said what he'd done, if he'd actually done anything, to have this influence. He had always shown an attitude of authority, a presence. "Boone don't play" was how someone put it. The sad truth is that prisoners rank each other according to the crimes they're convicted of, and murder is at the top. Perhaps knowing that he was in for murder caused other prisoners not to mess with him. And a thought snuck into my mind: Was he in a gang? Was his influence because of the power of gangs? I didn't ask.

All the while we talked, an officer walked around the tables and two other officers sat in a high glass booth keeping their eyes on the room. If you had to use the restroom, an officer unlocked it for you and waited outside until you came out. Though the visiting hours were supposed to be from 2:00 to 4:00 in the afternoon, our actual time was limited to an hour because we had lined up late, and Marell was delayed by the body checks.

I visited Foothills two or three times a month, depending on whether I had to work on Saturday. Because James normally did work each Saturday, he was limited to the visits that came around on Sundays. So I ended up driving up mostly with Sidnee, and less often with Kesia, whenever she came home from college.

Sidnee was usually my little comfort on the long drives back and forth. She never complained about using many Saturdays to visit her brother. I would be the one to decide if she didn't come on a given day because she never asked to stay home. And she was never antsy or misbehaved during these visits.

Years later, Sidnee and I talked about what was going on then. We both remembered my explanation that when someone does something bad, he has to go away. Even still, she told me, "Ma, you acted like nothing was wrong, like he was just there, but I never knew what was wrong." Then she said, "You always sugar-coated everything." And looking back, maybe I did. She was just a six-year-old girl, going on seven when she started coming with me to the prisons. It would not have been appropriate for her to know all of what brought Marell to where he was.

I wanted to shield her, yes, but having that sweet little girl visit her brother was also a way to steer him right. I wanted to keep their relationship going. I wanted Marell to be the young man he was as her big brother. "You are my right hand," he'd say to her. And I'd ask him, "What is Sidnee going to think of . . . " whenever something might take him into more trouble.

Early in his time at Foothills, Marell sometimes connived to let one of his female friends ride with me for a visit. Not Cheryl, because by then she was out of the picture. These were girls who had gone to school with him or were from the neighborhood, girls with names like Monique and Neka who had been a girlfriend for only a month or two in the past. When he went away, they surfaced and wanted to see him again. That was when I discovered that a man in prison is very attractive to some women, and Marell never lacked female visitors from his past who would show up from time to time.

One at a time, a girl would a catch a ride with me. We'd visit Marell together, then I'd give her the last fifteen minutes or so alone with him. A few times, the girl would wait in my car in the prison parking lot while I visited with my son, and then she'd come in. One way or another, I'd let her have some alone time with him. Like I said, I wanted to make him happy. At least this way he'd get a visitor beyond his family members. If he hadn't been in prison, he'd have been dating, and this was as close as he could get to that.

I allowed these girls to ride with me a few times, and then it got old. It was too much for me to run around Fayetteville picking them up before I left and dropping them off when I got back and trying to find something to talk about in the car. And who were they anyway? So I put a stop to bringing his old girlfriends to the prison. Enough was enough.

Once I got into a routine on these visits, I had my ritual that I started most often Thursday night. I'd get on my knees in prayer asking the Lord for strength to drive the distance. I'd usually shut down everything and everybody by Friday evening, and by Saturday morning I was completely concentrating on what I had to do: Breakfast before we left, making sure the car had enough gas, stopping for lunch before we got to the prison. Four hours there and four hours back. It was an all-day activity.

Sometimes the weather was a worry, especially in the winter. I would leave Fayetteville not knowing if the weather in the mountains would be bad or even good enough for me to drive all the way back. I went prepared to spend the night if I had to, but luckily I never did. One time, it was snowing so bad when I was leaving home that James begged me not to go. I said I had to, and he fussed that I didn't care what he said. I did care, but I felt like a soldier with a mission knowing what I had to do. That gave me strength.

While I worried about doing the drive, I can't remember a time when I was truly scared or fearful. And now, years later, I realize that I was blessed to have had a supervisor who always understood when I needed to take off for a visit. When I became supervisor, I generally gave more than forty hours a week-the place was like my second home-but I could often change my schedule. If I had to leave or take time off to do something for Marell, I could make up my hours later in the week. And I could be off on the days that prison visits were scheduled. Many people can't say that. They have to show up for work or lose a job, so the prisoner doesn't get a visit.

Marell was able to get a job in the Foothills kitchen. That's where there were the most jobs for inmates, except for the jobs cleaning some place like the library or computer room. He was a dishwasher and got paid around fifty cents for two or three hours work a day. The money went into his account. Even though his job involved very little pay, his performance went toward his record for good behavior and, hopefully, could help toward getting parole.

He needed every chance to improve his record. He was under a lot of stress to stay out of trouble. There were some very bad people at Foothills. Child molesters and murderers were men that Marell was with every day. One man was serving life for murder; his brother was serving two life sentences for murder in another prison. I rarely saw people who'd committed crimes like these in the visiting area because they hardly ever had any visitors, though the man whose brother was in another prison did have his mother visit. She'd come one Saturday to him and go the next Saturday to his brother. That mother surely had it a lot worse than I did.

Marell was writing more and more letters from Foothills and wrote that my phone calls and visits helped hold him together. "Every time I see or talk to you," he wrote in the spring of 1998, "I don't know what it is, but something inside me gives me a boost to keep going. Without you, I probably would've gave up a long time ago." This was just one of the many letters where Marell showed how grateful he was for my love, and the time and money I had spent to see him through. The more of this he expressed, the more eagerly I did things for him.

Yet I was worried by what he wrote. What was causing him so much stress? I wanted to know details, and they would come only in one-on-one conversation. So I went to visit him alone, and he was candid about the constant fighting and territorial wars that took place. Several inmates had been injured pretty badly. Then he confided how prejudiced the guards were. I had wanted to discuss this with him, but at the same time did not want to stir things up in his mind if it was just my imagination.

Since the very first visit, I noticed that the COs were not cordial. They barely spoke to visitors. Most of them had hard looks, as if to stare right through us. James noticed it too. It wasn't so much what they said as what they didn't say. When I'd greet them with "Hello," they wouldn't greet me back. I can't say this attitude was saved for just black visitors. I don't know.

But I do know that almost every guard was white. That did not surprise me when I realized that they mostly came from the Morganton area, which is over seventy-five percent white. And there was a lot of prejudice from COs toward prisoners like Marell. I mentioned that they would call him by his last name or his nickname, "Boone," but not always. Much of the time they'd forget the name and just call him and other black inmates "boy." Marell took this the same as being called "nigger." He felt they were taunting him. I was afraid these remarks would promote a riot. "Don't make this a race situation," I begged Marell, "just do your best to ignore them."

The guards made clear that they were in charge of what went on. Their attitude was, "I'm in control and you can't do anything about it. You have no defense." I know this is what prison life is about. The prisoners are not in control. That's what it's about. Yet I looked at the statements the COs made to Marell as threats. So did he.

And he did have many run-ins with the guards. He received write-ups for talking junk to them, for fighting with other inmates, and disobeying simple orders. He was also charged with being in unassigned areas. I'd say, "Son, why would you go to another cellblock to get your hair braided? Do not give the guards anything to charge you with." Yet every time he got in trouble, he was ready with an explanation for me. Boone had become a common name with the guards awful quick.

His circumstances added to my other stresses that spring of 1998. Little did he know, I was holding on by a thin thread, juggling visits to him with duties at home and at church and at my job.

And then there were girls' extra activities that needed my attention. Both of them were involved in pageants. Kesia's was sponsored by the Sigma Delta Theta Sorority where she had won an award for fundraising, and Sid was competing for the title of Young Miss Fayetteville. This meant finding the money for their dresses, getting hair done, and buying tickets for all of us to attend their events. Even though Sid didn't win, James and I were proud to watch her compete, and Kesia came home to cheer for her little sister.

As much as I love getting dressed up and going to formal events with my husband, I couldn't quite enjoy them because I was overwhelmed. I was torn between doing for my daughters and for my son. I tried to look happy and relaxed for all of them, but that was just a façade, especially during prison visits. I felt that if Marell knew my worries, they would bring him down. Everything seemed to be closing in on me, and if I was going to be good for anybody, I needed to take a break. So I decided to go to my family in Texas for the Easter holiday.

I depended on James and Sidnee to visit Marell, and Kesia also went to see him with two of her girlfriends from college. He really enjoyed talking and laughing with them. He acted so sure of himself, as if he could woo them, joking to me that they were not ready "for the tricks of the game," as he referred to his cool talk. Really, I thought? "*You* weren't ready for them." These were not the young, silly high school girls he was used to, and he felt the difference. Later, he did admit to me that he was shy with Kesia's friends. It was a humbling experience for him. Still, I was elated that she went to visit and took two of her friends. It showed me, and him too, that she wasn't ashamed of her brother, even if he was ashamed of himself.

I continued to be thankful for their visit and visits from any other relatives who made the effort to go to Foothills. Visits from my mother, brother, and sisters were limited because of the distance they had to travel from Texas, so each one of their visits was a treasure for Marell. All these people kept him in touch with family moments.

So did pictures of Sidnee's birthday, our trip to the State Fair and our Thanksgiving gathering at Aunt Earlene's and Uncle Charles's house. She was one of my favorite aunts. She and Uncle Charles talked about Marell at the dinner table frequently and recalled how they would take him and Kesia on fishing trips and little vacations every summer. Uncle Charles would always end his reminiscing by saying, "What good kids they were! I just hate it for him."

So 1998 rolled to an end, and each month in the new year brought more and more turmoil with Marell barely sliding by without write-ups. His letters described the flare-ups between him and other prisoners. He said that he had not been involved lately, but people were trying him, and he would *try* his best to avoid conflicts. What did he mean, "try his best"?

That question prompted my stern letters that carried a harsh tone. "Look, if you expect to get out of there, you have to abide by rules whether you like them or not. You proclaim this indescribable love for your family. Prove it then by staying out of trouble." Whether Marell was putting up a front for us or not, he claimed he entered a period of uplift because of letters and calls from young ladies that he knew. As time went by, I would understand why attention from these ladies was so important.

Each inmate has an assigned caseworker at the prison who addressed certain issues, like making appointments with a doctor or a dentist. Sometimes I would contact the caseworker myself. Some were helpful to me, but others let me know that Marell was an adult, and I had no business taking up for him. But Marell approached his caseworker himself when he asked to be moved from Foothills. He said it was a hardship for his mother and family to drive from Fayetteville to see him on the weekends. He asked the caseworker to address this matter in a letter to the warden. Marell looked for anything that would sway them. While he did want to make it easier for us, he also wanted to get away from the problems at Foothills.

During our Mother's Day visit, Marell reported that his caseworker had written the letter, but it was going to take a long time before he could transfer out of Foothills. Many inmates were ahead of him on a list to ship out. So Marell wrote his own letter to the warden to tell him that because of hardship and distance, his family needed him closer.

During his next appointment with the caseworker, Marell was surprised to find that he had been moved up on the list. At any moment, he could be shipped closer to us, though he didn't know where. This news put a huge grin on his face when he shared it with us at our next visit. It was wonderful to hear, but I was puzzled and asked how it could have happened. He responded, "I do not know. I am asking no questions. I give just praise to the Lord!" Yes, he needed to thank the Lord, because through it all, he was still so blessed. "Blessed" became our word for the rest of the year.

By the beginning of June, I was busy with summer camp at the rec center when my supervisor, B., called me to the phone saying it was Marell. My heart skipped a beat. We had agreed that calls to me at work would only be for emergencies. Something must have gone wrong. But no, he was calling to say he had been moved closer.

I burst out crying. "Why are you crying," Marell asked, "I thought the news would make you happy." And I was. My tears were for joy. I had been on my knees just two nights before and had spoken out loud to God saying I just could not travel those eight hours on Saturday anymore. It was killing me.

Marell laughed and said my prayers had been answered.

ELEVEN

Opportunities Lost

One morning, I was doing Sidnee's hair, when, out of the blue, she said she was so glad that Marell was in Lillington. That's where Harnett Correctional Institute is, just thirty miles from our home, and where Marell was since June 3, 1999.

I asked her why she was so happy, and she said because Marell was closer to us, and now he could go to school, when he hadn't been able to do that at Foothills. And here's the rest of what she said, which I put word for word in a letter to Marell: "She said she was so glad that you were doing good and if you keep believing in God you would be home soon. Marell, make her proud of you! We all love you!" Sidnee was a wise little eight-year-old. We used to say that she had come into the world already grown.

When I learned that Marell had left Foothills, I cried and cried. A part of me cried in rejoicing. In letters and phone conversations, I constantly reminded Marell that God had been so good to us. But I also cried because I was just plain scared. I had considered Foothills to be a transition, a temporary thing, not the real deal. Somehow having Marell move to another prison made it sink in like never before. He was in *prison* and *prison* would control our lives for years to come.

But Sidnee had been right about Harnett Correctional. Marell had many good influences there and opportunities for positive direction in his life.

First off, the whole atmosphere at Harnett was different than Foothills, more relaxed. The guards were friendlier and talked openly to us when we checked in for visits. And during visits, the guards would walk around, and Marell introduced us to several of them. Some of the COs commented that Marell was well-mannered and questioned how he could have gotten involved in such a crime. I made the point to Marell that seeing what kind of family he came from, the staff greeted us with respect and had high expectations for him.

The rules for visitation at Harnett made things easier on us too. Marell put names-ten if I remember correctly-on his visitors' list. These people included his family members and friends, some of them Marell's female friends. I felt particularly proud when my family traveled all the way from Texas to see Marell. Whenever my sisters Andrea and Sheri planned a vacation, it always included a visit with him. That way they got to see him at least once a year, and Andrea would bring her children, who were just little tots, so that Marell would get to know his cousins. Over time, Marell's rec center coach, and my uncles Felton and Junior went to see Marell. I welcomed their visits, because these were men, along with James, my brother, and my father (who also came up from Texas), who could motivate and influence Marell positively.

Daddy had retired from the United States Army in 1976 as a Master Sergeant and Green Beret in the10th Special Forces Airborne Division. He'd served three tours of duty in Vietnam and received awards as a master parachutist, marksman, and sharpshooter, and for his work in military intelligence. He was not argumentative or a big talker, but when he did talk, you listened, and he talked army all the time and preached making something out of your life.

He was also very stern and believed in order. When I was growing up, I was the dishwasher in the family, and if he found just one dish in the cabinet that wasn't cleaned right, I had to take everything out and wash all the dishes again. I routinely told this story to my children because I wanted them to get the same message my Daddy had taught me: Follow through, do a job right the first time, and you will not have to repeat it.

My father doted on the males in the family, and Marell wanted to be a good person in his "Pa Pa's" eyes. Sometimes Marell asked us to keep certain things from my father. He was embarrassed for Daddy to know when he got written up or sent to the hole. "Why does he have to know?" Marell would ask me. I would tell Marell, if there was any one in the family he should take the time to call and contact, it should be my daddy.

At certain times, the visitors' list had to be changed. If someone turned out to be a no-show, that person's name would be removed from the list and replaced with another. But once you were on the list, you didn't have to call the prison ahead to make an appointment for a visit. People on the list would call me before going to see Marell to be sure there was room for them. So it never happened that we got to Harnett and couldn't get in because there were too many visitors. And every Sunday after church, we'd immediately leave in our dressy church clothes so that we could arrive on time. It was a regular part of my life, just like showing up for my job at Spivey.

Our own first visit was one to write home to Mama about. It took James, Sidnee and myself an easy thirty-five minutes to drive to the Harnett facility. The visit was outside on a beautiful June day. We couldn't bring Marell any kind of food, so I had money for the snack machines. There was no recourse if you lost money in them so I quickly learned to bring $6.00 to $8.00 in exact change.

A regular feature of every visit was the opportunity to have our pictures taken. These had to be pre-paid by Marell through his prison account. The amount was around $2.00 for each picture that was taken by a designated inmate. I assume he was picked because he had demonstrated good behavior and didn't have his own visitors at that time, so he was happy to have something to do that was different from his routine. Marell would joke with him that I was a photographer and could give him some pointers.

During that first visit, the line for picture taking was long, but I did not mind at all. When it was our turn, I told the inmate the best way to hold the camera. We took two prints. One was with the whole family and the second picture was of Marell and Sidnee. He wanted to keep them both. But I told him I'd make a copy of the one with the four of us and send it back to him. And I did just that. What a picture that was to show off!

I still saw Marell as my good-looking young boy. "Hey, good-lookin'!" I'd sometimes call out to him. By the time he arrived at Harnett, he'd grown to almost six feet tall, but he was not much heavier than he had been in when he went away in 1996. He had cut his hair nice and trim, and he was trying to grow a little beard under his chin. "Look, Pops, look what I got," he'd say to James pointing to his chin. And we'd joke back at him, "What? That little bit of fuzz?"

The only thing that made him seem more adult now was that he wore cologne during every visit. We could smell it immediately when he walked in to the visiting room. He prided himself on taking a shower and splashing on this scent before seeing us, even if it made him late. Sometimes I'd fuss at him for taking time away from our visit. "You know we'd take you any old way," I'd tell him.

But he wanted to be as clean and sharp as possible when he saw his family. I think he did that for himself as much as for us. This was one of the few ways he could be the same person he had been at home, where he was always neat and never came to the dinner table without cleaning up. He took to heart our expectations about what was respectful. And now it tickled him when I commented about his appearance and how good and clean he smelled.

Looking at the pictures taken during visits to Marell at Harnett, I realize that someone could be tricked into thinking that he wasn't really in prison. We'd be posed in front of a pretty backdrop of a waterfall or a beach that changed from time to time. It looked as if we were on a family trip somewhere-no guards or barbed wire or ugly prison buildings in sight. Marell's uniform of khaki pants and a white tee shirt was what was issued to medium custody prisoners, but khakis and tee shirts were the kind of clothes you see men wearing everywhere, all the time. Marell and Sid were hugging in some pictures; in others, our arms were around each other-James, and me and both girls, or Uncle Felton or Uncle Junior, just your typical family gathering after church on Sunday. Even though it wasn't.

Marell eagerly attended classes that were offered at Harnett by instructors from Central Carolina Community College. Each semester, after he received his grade report, he would send it home. That made us so proud. I knew that if he felt good about himself, it would improve his whole attitude. While he was at Harnett, he completed courses in auto mechanics, communications, and, surprisingly, he got a cooking certificate too. He became very interested in carpentry, and that entailed classes in blueprinting, residential planning, and cabinet making.

He also took a course in brick masonry. When that was completed in the spring of 2001, he announced he would be having a graduation ceremony. We even got an official graduation invitation. Well really, it was just a description that the prison sent of what would take place at the ceremony. Only two persons could attend. No cameras or recording devices, no contact with an inmate, no gestures, and no sounds. Still, it was a real graduation with the cap and gown, and I went to bragging and letting family and friends know. My son was graduating!

Around the same time, we had another graduation in the family. May 20, 2001, was Kesia's big day. I say "big day," but there were really two big days. The first one was within the department of her major, Communications, where she received a certificate. Then the next day, Kesia got her diploma at the ceremony in Kenan Stadium, where UNC plays home football games.

Events like this make me nervous because I always want everything to go just right. James, Sid, and me, my mother and Aunt Rutha, Kesia's boyfriend, and "B." (my supervisor from work who by now was like a member of the family), we all had to be on time. When we got to Chapel Hill, we were joined by relatives from my father's family who had driven down from Maryland.

I had made a big sign with the words "CONGRATS KESIA" to hold up in the stands. James declared that someone in security would surely make me pull it down, but turns out I was not the only one with that idea. Plenty of signs and banners were raised to celebrate graduates. Many families were proud to see their loved ones graduate from this prestigious university. What joy we all felt!

Of course Marell couldn't be with us, so he had asked for me to take a lot of pictures. But he didn't need to ask because I was set to do everything possible to make him feel part of our celebration. I videoed the entire ceremony, moving up and down the bleachers so I could capture every angle. After the tassels were turned, I rushed onto the field to snap more pictures of Kesia with her friends.

I was so happy to help Kesia celebrate. She deserved it. We had always known she could excel in anything she put her mind to. Her grades had been good, and she had worked hard to get to this day. But there would be many days of hard work ahead because she was going right to law school in the fall.

Marell was also smart, but in his own way. He was curious about all sorts of things. About this time, he became intrigued about stocks, bonds, mutual funds, and different types of real estate investments, so I sent him books-they had to be mailed straight from the publishing company-on these subjects.

Every now and then he would share his dreams about investments when he got out. He'd often tell us that we should get a loan to invest in real estate. But he really did not have a clue about how few the opportunities were for getting a profitable loan. The only loans we had on our mind were the ones for Kesia's schooling. Still, when James described his woes about the little business he'd started, Marell assured him that he had the perfect business plan for him.

To supplement income from James's main job at Cumberland County Schools, he'd started doing lawn care for neighbors, co-workers, and small businesses. This part-time gig grew and grew from doing three or four yards on weekends to having yards he did during the week when he got off from work.

The expansion of Williams Lawn Care seemed to take all of his spare time, but James loved it, and we needed the extra money. He began to talk about this becoming a permanent business, an investment that he could call his own when he retired from the school system. James even said that when Marell got out, he could work with him. Marell would joke and tell his dad that he would bring fresh ideas to the business. Marell even sent him a packet with business plans. James was pretty set in his ways of doing things, yet he welcomed Marell's ideas.

Many blessings came Marell's way while he was at Harnett. I learned that several of the men from our church served in the prison ministry there. They would provide Bible study and opportunities for prisoners to commit to Christ and be baptized. "Lord, you are steady in opening ways for my child," I would pray in thanksgiving.

While I did not want to push Marell about attending services every week, I surely reminded him. When I went to church each Sunday, I asked the brethren if they'd had the chance to talk with my son during their prison visits. It warmed my heart if I found out that Marell had interacted with them.

Unfortunately this didn't happen often, and soon Marell made excuses why he missed the Bible study. This was his loss, but it made me sad. I hoped for anyone or anything that might motivate and encourage him in the right direction.

There were also two COs from Fayetteville who spent time giving Marell motivational talks. One of them was a religious man, which I took as another of Marell's many blessings. And I was also happy when I found out about Vincent, an inmate who was also serving time in Harnett.

Vincent's sentence was so long I didn't think he'd ever leave prison, and I know many people considered his punishment overly harsh. Still he never became hard-core or bitter. He was calm, followed the rules, and the COs recognized him as a role-model inmate. He also earned the respect of the other inmates. It's not an everyday thing that a prisoner is respected by the COs *and* the inmates.

Vincent managed because he had found the Lord. He figured out how to make something positive out of all that was negative. He welcomed and encouraged Marell, who admired and listened to him. He was inspirational, and I want him to know that I appreciate it, so even today, I continue to send Vincent cards to let him know we pray for him and are grateful for all he tried to do. He writes back to thank us for our prayers and says he prays for us too. We have to believe, he says; that is where we gain our strength, trusting in God.

And then there was Devon. Explaining his relationship with Marell can get complicated. His mother, Rhea, and Marell knew each other during their early years of high school, though I never even heard her name then. They had gone their separate ways, but when Marell went to jail, she started visiting him, and by that time she had a baby boy named Devon. She brought the little fellow with her when she visited, and Marell decided to adopt Devon, not legally of course, but verbally, Marell telling Rhea that he vowed to be the boy's dad.

James and I thought this didn't make a bit of sense. To make that promise while he was facing years of prison and had nothing to offer but love? We hated that a child had to get to know the only dad in his life this way. I wanted to tell Marell this was a stupid idea, but James talked me out of it because the relationship with Devon brought happiness to Marell, who referred to Devon as his "little man." Seeing himself in the role of a dad would be another motivation to stay out of trouble and have something like a normal life. So we eased our minds on the subject. From time to time, we would take Devon to family gatherings and even brought him with us to visits with our son. If Devon did not come with us, his mother visited faithfully with the boy to support Marell.

I learned from Marell that inmates would point out to each other who had women coming to see them. The way I looked at it, prisoners are always needing to prove themselves, and these visits were a way to send a signal: I'm a man with a woman.

You hear about the terrible things that go on between men in prison. You'd hear rumors about certain men when they got out, that they'd turned gay or at least they'd been "gay for the stay." This subject of manhood is a sensitive one among prisoners, worth fighting and catching a charge over. After Marell had been in for many years, I picked my time carefully to ask had he ever been approached by another prisoner. He said they all knew he was straight, and they'd get a beatdown if they tried anything. "You wouldn't dare touch me" was the attitude he sent off. I took him at his word and never thought or talked about that topic again.

During my drives to the prison, I used to think long and hard about what I'd talk to Marell about that day. I'd think of real life subjects like writing checks or new inventions with telephones. So and so went to college and did such and such. Things we take for granted are not what prisoners talk about with each other. Their conversation is very confined, and much of it is not uplifting. Marell would say, "This is a different world, Ma." When I asked him what he talked to other prisoners about, he said he put a limit on what he said. He didn't talk much about his sisters because he didn't want any of the inmates drooling over them.

Despite all that was positive going on at Harnett, it was still prison. Within six months of Marell arriving, I saw his attitude begin to change. At first I had trouble figuring out whether this change was for the good or not.

There was a calmness about him. He was comfortable. He had built a connection because many of his co-inmates were from Fayetteville. Some he knew before, some he'd even gone to school with. But they formed cliques and rallied in fights. They acknowledged him during our visits as though he was *the man*, someone important. This was big to Marell, but it was not good.

Marell was entertaining negative involvements. He told us that he ran card games. Playing cards is not an infraction, and I knew he'd done that at Foothills. I looked at it naively, as an innocent pastime. But not 'til he was in Harnett did I understand how these card games could be a problem.

I never played cards for money. But James pointed out that if there were cards, betting was going on, and with betting, anything could go wrong. That's when trouble starts, and the exchange of money with actual dollars and cents is seriously against the rules. Once Marell slipped and admitted that money was sometimes exchanged to consummate various deals. When I asked what that meant, he stayed vague. He said he just saw this as a way of collecting extra canteen money.

It seemed many things were happening that the COs had no control over or ignored. For example, prisoners looking to get drunk saved fruit, added sugar to it, and fermented it in their cells to make wine. Marell knew that telling me he did this would lead to a good fussing. Did he ever get drunk, or high? I'd love to say "No, never," to say that he knew how I felt about this and stayed away from those things. He had never come home drunk or high when he was in high school, and at each visit, I'd look hard at his eyes, and I can say I never saw him high.

Then there was an incident that began on June 24, 2002. Marell was playing basketball, something he did a lot when he wasn't occupied with his job in the kitchen or his courses. If prisoners didn't have anything better to do, they could spend the whole day in the yard playing basketball.

On this particular day, he was randomly pulled for a urine test. This was routine. Prisoners never knew when they would be tested for controlled substances like marijuana, cocaine, and opioids. His sample was frozen and examined on June 28th. When the results came back from the lab on July 8th, they clearly stated he was negative for marijuana or any controlled substance. But the lab also stated that the sample *might* have been "adulterated" or "diluted."

So on that same day, Marell was charged with an A99 offense. Class A disciplinary offenses are the most serious offenses a North Carolina prisoner can be charged with, an A99 the worst. It was equal to a felony charge given for assaulting another inmate or attempting to escape or a whole list of other similar offenses.

This seemed crazy to me, so I jumped in to help. I called Harnett Correctional and made sure I spoke to the highest-ranking person on duty. That was a captain, and he was cordial. I asked him to clarify whether Marell's test was positive or negative. "It was negative," he answered, "it was not contaminated, but it was diluted, with no consistency with normal gravity in the body." I questioned how Marell could have diluted his urine if an officer was standing in front of him while he dispensed it into the container. The captain had no answer, but he did say that the A99 charge was a mistake and would be changed to a lesser one. By July 17th, Marell was charged with an A13, which is to "refuse to submit to a drug test or Breathalyzer test, or interfere with the taking of such tests."

The difference between the A99 and A13 offenses seemed pretty big to me, but the punishment for any A Class offense can be the same: 60 days in the hole, 180 days loss of visitation, telephone, and canteen, and a loss of 40 days of "good time." That means a loss of days of good behavior that could be subtracted from time at the end of a sentence. So when I had finished my conversation with that captain at Harnett Correctional, I thanked him, but I let him know I was not satisfied with his answers. I planned to take the matter further. Through a person who worked at North Carolina Department of Prisons and had heard me talk about Marell, his situation came to the attention of an official. That person began a thorough investigation into Marell's A13 charge.

Once an inmate receives a charge, paper work goes from one desk to another before a hearing, and a few days before Marell's hearing, I had a tough decision. My family reunion was coming up in Texas. Should I go or not? I would only be gone a little more than a week, but when it came time to leave, there was no knowing if it would be days or weeks between seeing Marell when I returned. Part of me wanted to stay close to my son, but another part of me knew that I had to be with my daughters and husband and my parents and sisters.

So I went to Texas, even though it felt like a hard task to enjoy fellowship with family with my heavy heart. I prayed and welcomed my family to pray with me that everything would work out. I let Marell call three times a day so he could talk with whoever was in my mother's house. I promised her I would pay for every call that she accepted. I agreed to anything to calm Marell from thinking about how much time he might be without contact.

When Marell didn't call on July 23rd, we all knew he'd gone to the hole. At his hearing that day, he had been found guilty of the A13. Still, a piece of my heart was calm. I was waiting to hear what the findings would be from the North Carolina Department of Prisons.

On the 30th I got a letter from Marell. It was marked urgent all over the envelope. Enclosed was a copy of his appeal statement. "Today I was found guilty of a charge that I did not and had no intentions of committing," he wrote. And then in three pages, he laid out what happened, starting with the day he was pulled for the drug test: "I was asked to put on a pair of latex gloves, enter the restroom and drop my pants and boxers to my knees, lift my shirt, and face the supervising officer as I urinated in the provided cup. He watched carefully from start to finish." This particular CO had the reputation of being so thorough that he made drug testing "inmate tamper-proof." Marell continued his letter: "I then handed the cup with the urine sample to Officer Henley, and with the cup in his hand I proceeded to place on the lid and tightly seal the cup. I then initialed the cup and other paper work involved in the procedure. I did not tamper or in any way dilute the sample."

Perhaps the urine was diluted because of all the water he'd been drinking while he was playing basketball in ninety-five-degree heat, Marell stated. Or perhaps the sample was contaminated or diluted because it had been frozen for four days before it was defrosted and analyzed. Or perhaps there was an error at the lab: "I hope you can relate to me as being a person and not just a convicted felon. Because just like I made a mistake, it's also possible that the system can make one, the way it has in my situation." Then he concluded: "My appeal to this situation, is not to criticize the staff at Harnett Corr. or the staff at the results lab, but to challenge the decision that they made."

Marell had already sent his appeal to the proper channels, but he also wanted me to make copies to send to the listed addresses. Then he added:

"But I guess God puts you in situations to make you stronger and teach you patience." I never expected him to make statements like that. Whenever he did, it was startling, like him coming up for air with God. He ended the letter saying, "when you get back and you start making phone calls, please don't stop bugging or calling them until they give you some answers."

Later that same day, there was a phone call. An automated voice said, "You have a collect call from Harnett Correctional Institution." Marell couldn't call from the hole, so this meant something awful had happened. Some prison official was calling to give me bad news. And then I heard Marell's voice, and it was music to my ears. He was out of the hole. All charges would be dropped. A couple of weeks later, a letter from the North Carolina Department of Correction confirmed the decision to dismiss the disciplinary charge against "inmate Williams." Not only was Marell's charge dropped—so were charges against other men who'd been sent to the hole as a result of those drug tests on June 24th.

Something had gone wrong that day, and the official at the DOC had made it right. I was proud of the way Marell had handled himself. I'll never know if my call to the captain or having a contact in the Department of Correction helped. But I was glad I could do my part and worried about those inmates who had no one outside the prison to fight for them. Maybe what I'd done had helped them too.

I had trusted the COs at Harnett when Marell got there. I believed they were going to take care of him. And now I had to wonder, did they not care that being wrongly accused would keep the inmates from their family? Did COs make up their own laws with each case? One thing I had no question about: They wouldn't like anyone outsmarting them, going over their heads, and getting a charge dropped. "You better watch your back," I warned Marell.

Every prison performs a routine custody review twice a year. That's when officials determine if an inmate is assigned to the correct level of custody: close, medium, minimum I, minimum II or minimum III. A prisoner who has obeyed rules and meets requirements can be moved to less restrictive custody, but if a prisoner is believed to be a risk to the public or other inmates or staff, he is sent to close custody. In some prisons, inmates wear different uniforms according to their level of custody. Other prisons house inmates at a specific level, like close custody or minimum security prisons.

But an inmate doesn't arrive at a new prison with a clean slate. Uncle Felton warned Marell, "Your paper trail will stay with you for the rest of your life." And so nothing positive came out of Marell's custody review after he was cleared of that A13 charge for tampering with a urine sample. He had come to Harnett with four infractions left over from his time in Foothills, and in a few years, he had six more. Depending on the charge, his canteen, phone calls, or visits were taken away. Some infractions got him time in the hole. In fact, he spent three months in the hole during 2003. And by 2004, he had a total of fifteen infractions.

Whenever I heard that he had gotten into trouble, I became emotional to the point of tears. I never got used to it. But Marell got used to writing letters apologizing that he had upset the family. He would ask me to please not cry. In one letter, he stated that when I cried, it broke him down because I was his strength. He stated that when I weakened, his strength weakened as well. "Cut the crap," I told him. I was worn out with him doing things he had to apologize for. Marell was aging my soul with each infraction.

But Kesia, her life soothed my soul. Thank God for her!

On the morning of May 1, 2004, I could not help but smile when I reflected back to a day twenty-two years before. That day, when I picked my almost four-year-old daughter up from preschool, she announced she wanted to be a lawyer when she grew up. I laughed and said to myself, "She does not know what in the world she is talking about."

But throughout school and college, she never wavered. In fact, her brother's situation had made her more determined. She even wrote in her law school application letter that she wanted to be the voice for people who get caught up in bad situations. And now, here she was, about to graduate from law school.

Most of the friends and members of our family who had celebrated Kesia's graduation from college-the people who had stood by us in the worst of times-were with us now on another exciting, proud, and very emotional day. During that ceremony it began to drizzle, but that did not last long, and we didn't care, watching Kesia walk up to the stage and get her diploma. Afterward, James presented her with flowers, and of course I took pictures. Well, well. Our daughter had received a Juris Doctor!

It was a joy for Kesia to introduce us to her professors and classmates. They spoke so highly of her and admired how she kept up with all her courses in law school while she worked to help pay her bills. And there had been so many of them: rent on an apartment, car payments, and living expenses in addition to her tuition and fees.

After the ceremonies, we had a party at the Italian restaurant where Kesia had waitressed part-time for three years. We decorated the place in the North Carolina Central University colors, burgundy and grey. We had set up a table to show off Kesia's cake, her cap and gown picture, and her diploma. People put their gifts and cards on that table or pinned cash to a money tree that I'd made out of Styrofoam.

Here we were celebrating Kesia's accomplishments, and she turned the party around to celebrate James and me, saying how important we were in her life and thanking us for helping her get to where she was that day. She had set up a projector and showed pictures that made us laugh, and definitely made us cry—pictures of her growing up and moments with Marell, and some of my grandmother, who had been so important in Kesia's life, and other pictures of Kesia's childhood and awards. Many of our guests spoke in praise of her, and she said how much my support had meant to her. Yes, I cried, happy tears, and then the rest of the evening was filled with laughs, good food, and memorable stories, such the one about Kesia's decision when she was just four years old to become a lawyer.

March of 2005 was the start of bad things for Marell. I know God had a plan, but it did not include a whole lot of smiling. Marell had gotten in trouble for fighting and his fate was to be thirty days in the hole and ninety days with no visitation or canteen. Until all paperwork was in, he was allowed regular visits and calls, and he could continue his classes.

Marell had started business studies, but the courses had been a little harder than he was used to. Several times he became discouraged and said he wanted to quit. Marell knew how I felt about starting something and not fulfilling it: "Do not quit. Things that you struggle for are worth the struggle in the end." His classes were sometimes on Saturdays, which were normal visiting days. For that reason, the prison allowed visits during the week. I had just had sent money for Marell's account and visited him on a Thursday, the day before I got a strange phone call.

On Friday, March 18th, an operator announced a collect call from the prison. But it was not my son. "Now who did you say you were again?" I asked.

Another inmate was calling. He spoke timidly and said Marell had asked him to call. "He wants to let you know that he got into some trouble, and they have taken him to Harnett County Jail. He will have court at 9:00 on Monday morning." That's all he knew or, at least, that was how the caller left it.

My head nearly exploded. What? He was in prison and they took him to *jail*? I'd never heard of such a thing. He was already in trouble for fighting. Was this about something different?

I called James, and he told me to calm down until we found out everything. Then I called the prison and asked for a captain on duty. As I held for him, I thought how the staff had come to know me by name. Was my name one that they dreaded to hear? Did they wish there was some way they could avoid speaking to me? At that moment, I did not care what they thought of me. I just needed someone to explain why my son had gone from the *prison* to the *jail*.

The officer politely told me that Marell had been charged with drug possession—*drug possession*—and that I would be able to attend his first appearance in court on Monday. The captain also assured me that Marell would be given the chance to call me after getting processed at the jail.

James had not been home from work long when the phone rang. It was a collect call again, this time from Marell himself. I stood right in front of James as he questioned him. After a few minutes, James gave me the phone. I was not as calm as my husband had been. I wanted answers.

How did you get drugs? Who gave them to you? How did you get caught? "Ma, it's just crazy the way it happened" was the answer he gave me. I realized it would be in his best interest not to talk about this on the phone. So I assured him we would be in court on Monday, and then I hung up and cried for hours, trying to understand. Why would Marell get involved with drugs? I came up with no reason. He had money on his books. What else would he need?

When Marell called again on the weekend, he described his woes this way. He had been on a break from class, minding his own business, on his way to chill out in the yard when an inmate asked him to deliver a perfectly normal looking brown paper bag to someone. Why not? He was going to the yard anyway. But he hadn't taken two steps before correctional officers surrounded him. They opened the brown paper bag and found three small bags of cocaine.

During this call, I never questioned that Marell was remorseful. He said he hated that he worried me this way. But those words did not give me any relief. That relief would not come until I could hear fully what happened to make Marell get involved with stupid moves.

I never wondered if he had been doing a friend a favor. Marell had told me many times, "Ma, there are no friends here, just associates. Everyone is out for himself. I always sleep with one eye open." So why had Marell taken that bag? Had he been tricked? There had to have been something in it for him. Was he being offered something? Perhaps somebody pressured him. Perhaps he owed somebody something. If he was being pressured or owed something, he didn't tell me then, or ever. And why had this happened just now? Marell had accumulated points with days of good behavior towards the possibility of being sent to a medium security prison. In a place like that, he would be under less supervision and could become eligible for certain kinds of work, like being assigned to a highway crew or a yard company. But now he might lose his chance to be moved from Harnett Correctional to a better place.

When Monday came, James and I took off from work to drive to Harnett County. We prepared for the morning traffic and left in time to feel our way to the courthouse. When we entered, it was packed. We had been lucky to get in, but it was a tight squeeze. People were standing against the walls of the courtroom, and pretty soon people were waiting outside to come in. I wondered if all these people were going to fit in that small courtroom. Weren't there any fire codes against overcrowding? How would those people in the hallway hear a loved one's name when it was called?

When the clerk called Marell's name, two officers-one male and one female-walked my handcuffed, devastated-looking son through a side door to the front of the court. Marell answered, "Present," then walked to the holding area with the officers.

A few minutes passed, names were called, people were taking pleas, and I noticed that the female officer who had accompanied Marell was heading toward the back of the courtroom. She was an older, white woman who didn't seem very strong. I wondered how she stood up to prisoners when she needed to. I assumed that she was on her way to the restroom, so I stood up and followed her without a plan as to what I would say. When I opened the restroom door, she looked at me kindly, like she could have hugged me, and spoke first.

"Mrs. Williams, you just visited him," she said. She had seen me at the prison the previous Thursday, the day before the incident, though I had not noticed her. She was one of the COs who knew me by name, but she didn't seem to want to avoid me.

"I left him money for his canteen items."

"I know. And I knew you would follow me in here to get answers," she said. "It was unfortunate that this happened to Marell. You need to find out about this." She wished us well, then stated that she could lose her job for talking to me. So I thanked her, and our conversation ended, but before leaving the restroom, I had the feeling that this incident had been a set-up. If that was true—who set him up and why—I would never know.

Back in the courtroom, it took about an hour and a half before Marell was called from the holding area. The judge read the charges: "Possession of cocaine with the intent to distribute and sell," and then he added, "You're looking at the possibility of a ten-year sentence per each one ounce bag." If these thirty years ran consecutively, in addition to the twenty he was in for, that would add up to a life sentence.

When the judge asked Marell how he would plead, he answered, "Not guilty." And in response to the judge's question about an attorney, Marell asked for one to be appointed. Then a distinguished-looking man wearing a suit stood up and nodded at the judge. The next court date was set for April 12th. Officers led Marell out the same door they had entered by. He was going back to jail before returning to Harnett Correctional.

The man who nodded, the attorney, walked toward a different door, and James and I followed him outside the courthouse where my Uncle Junior, one of the men in our family who regularly visited Marell in prison, joined us. He'd driven from his home in Moncure, North Carolina, about a half an hour away, to support us that hard day. The three of us introduced ourselves to the attorney whose name was Andrew Newsome.

Uncle Junior commented about the boots Mr. Newsome was wearing, something that my uncle would notice because he himself wore snakeskin belts and alligator shoes. Uncle Junior dressed very well. Everything had to match. He owned a construction company and did hard work, but he was the neatest man I knew, and I never saw him in anything but clean clothing. But when he and the attorney started talking about belts and boots, I thought to myself, this is not why we're here. So I brought the subject back around with a request to meet Mr. Newsome in his office.

By the middle of the following week, when Marell wrote me with information about the attorney, I had already found out about him from several people. Marell was blessed to have received a regular attorney, not a public defender. But this was not *pro bono* work. Because there are not enough public defenders to cover every case, the state pays private attorneys to take some cases on. Marell was lucky to have been assigned a top attorney dealing with drug offenses. I was relieved that the lawyer working on Marell's case knew what he was doing.

We visited our son in prison the following Sunday, and James had some harsh words for him, chastising him like he was a little boy. I began to cry the same way I did when Marell got in trouble as a kid, but I dared not interrupt or speak my peace. I knew Marell needed that reality check from his father. If it had been me talking, Marell would have tried to defend himself or give explanations. But he kept quiet without a word until James finished.

The following Monday, Kesia joined me to meet with Mr. Newsome. He seemed straight up with us and expressed that it was unusual to meet with an adult client's family. He went as far as to say that Marell was an adult and should be able to hold his own. I almost took offense at that statement and let the attorney know we were a close-knit family that stood by each other. My role as a mother was to help my son.

Mr. Newsome was impressed that Kesia had completed law school and was preparing to take the North Carolina bar exam. She led the rest of our conversation with her questions, and we learned his strategic plan for the defense. He would try to get Marell's sentence for the drug charge to run concurrent with his existing sentence, and he would be sure to get the right judge. These things happen all the time, he said. The whole matter was routine to him, when it was so strange to me. It was worrying me sick.

The attorney visited Marell once he was back in prison and spoke to him about Kesia. Marell appreciated all that she had done for him, but he realized that it would be hard to prove his version of the incident because he was not giving up names. I know that the worst thing you can be in prison is a snitch. Mr. Newsome told Marell the same as he'd told us. If he could not get him off, then he'd try to get the sentence to run concurrent. Marell said he wouldn't settle for less.

Marell wrote all this in a letter that I read as I did all his letters, as if I was hearing his voice. I could just hear him bluntly saying: "I won't settle for less." I hated that attitude, like he had control over the way things would go. Soon after I read this letter, I talked tough to him in a phone call: "Son, you are possibly looking at thirty *more* years. Guilty or not, your poor choices have got to stop. Take this seriously. What a mess you have created! Not only a mess for you but for the family, too. You are a pitiful example of an older brother. This is a shame that Sidnee has to hear about all of your nonsense."

Matter of fact, we hadn't told Sidnee about these drug charges. From the time that Marell was arrested, we'd kept things from her. I believed the less she knew, the more I was protecting her. We didn't talk about his situation in front of her, or if we did, we'd use a kind of code, thinking she wouldn't understand. When she asked why he didn't come home, we simply told her that when someone does wrong, he has to go away. For years, she seemed satisfied with that answer. She never asked the specific, important question: "What did he do that he had to go to prison?" and I didn't feel a need to tell her. But if she had asked, how would I have answered? I didn't want to discredit her number one brother in her eyes. Yet I knew how much Marell loved her and how ashamed he'd be if she heard all that was going on in prison, especially his trouble over a drug charge. I tried to motivate him with the threat of telling Sidnee or Devon and my daddy about things Marell didn't want them to know.

So while we waited to hear his fate over the drug charges, the prison disciplinary board decided Marell's punishment for fighting. He would go to the hole for thirty days. This would be the end his business courses.

As usual, Marell prepared for going into solitary by emptying his cell of any personal items. There was never any going back to the same cell or even the same cellblock. When he would come out of solitary and return to the general prison population, he would have to establish who he was with a whole new group of inmates. That was another reason Marell hated going into the hole.

So he'd box up his few personal possessions, like the thermals I'd sent him. During the winter, it was very cold in the cells because Harnett Correctional was an old facility. The heating system wasn't up to par, and of course, there were no air conditioners during the summer. Marell would also send home the letters and pictures he'd accumulated. He probably received ten letters a week from different people as well as pictures that girls were sending him. I'd send him pictures of events and people at home, hoping to bring his mind to a happy place.

By the fifth of April, Marell was writing from the hole. He acknowledged that he would miss visiting me on Mother's Day, and without canteen privileges, he couldn't even buy a card to send me. But more often than buying a card, he would sometimes make a card for me or have a talented inmate draw me something.

It always amazed me the kind of talent prisoners had. They'd use anything—candy wrappers, paper napkins, cleaning cloths—for their art. I'm sure Marell must have paid for their work somehow and that prison officials knew that inmates didn't do this artwork for nothing. One particularly beautiful gift Marell gave me while he was in prison is a picture of me done by an inmate on some cloth (a cleaning cloth, I think) that he stretched over a piece of 11 x 14 cardboard. That inmate based his painting on a photograph that I'd sent Marell. He explained how this inmate heated Starburst or Now and Later candy wrappers, then rubbed their pink and red and blue colors onto a pencil, and created a chalk-like material that he used in the painting. When he was finished, he covered his painting in the plastic wrap he'd gotten from the kitchen so it wouldn't smudge. It's a good likeness, and I've preserved it in a frame.

On April 12th, James and I traveled to the courthouse for Marell's hearing. We sat cramped up for about forty-five minutes, but Marell didn't appear in court. There was no need, because when his name was called, Mr. Newsome stepped toward the bench and asked for a continuance. The judge honored the request and announced yet another court date. Then the attorney made eye contact with us and motioned to the back doors where we met up with him. He said he planned to request more continuances until he got enough information on the case to proceed.

Meanwhile Marell was writing from the hole every week. It gave me peace to know that he was away from the other inmates and that he felt good enough to continue communication with his family.

I realized that when he went to the hole for the first time, I was so fearful about how he would react during weeks without human contact. Would he break down and lose his sanity? Would he quit on himself? But now I compared solitary to the time-out I'd give kids at the rec center when they misbehaved. It was a chance for space away from others, a place to think. A mother with a son in prison finds peace in the strangest ways.

Meanwhile, we were practically going crazy waiting to know his punishment for the drug offense. And then, we got word from his caseworker that when he left Harnett Correctional it would be for another medium custody prison.

Were we happy!

But not for long. The warden quickly overturned that decision. Marell would be sent to a maximum security prison.

While he waited at Harnett to be moved there, wherever it would be, he remained in solitary. I was on pins and needles, wondering every day if I'd get a call from him in a new place. But meanwhile, in his letters, he seemed okay about what he was facing, even though he was going to a close custody facility: "Ma, it will be a fresh start for me. Please, Ma, please don't break down because IT'S NOT THAT BAD!" He wrote that in all caps.

Easily said, I thought. He had no clue what was coming. He was about to make a shockwave move where what little freedom he had in prison would be even more limited. Or maybe he did know what was coming and tried to act calm for my wellbeing. Because I feared what I was about to go through, I called his caseworker to learn from someone other than Marell what we should expect. Though I got no comfort from her, I did get a second point of view. I understood more clearly about the terms of Marell's continuances for the drug charges and about his transfer to a maximum security facility.

My next few letters to Marell were strictly to motivate him: "Keep the faith and remember we are in this together! God will not put more on us than we can take!" Now it was *me* trying to put forward something positive for *him*.

In my heart, I wondered if I had fallen short in my faith. Had I stopped relying on the Lord as I should? I focused again and reminded myself how my family was blessed even through these trials and tribulations. We were going through this for a reason. So I actually stopped and reflected on the fact that even though things had gone so bad, when things were good at Harnett, they had been very good.

On May 16th, while Marell was still in the hole waiting for whatever would come next, he wrote: "Your son is much smarter than a lot of people even know and to be honest with you, I'm going to go a long way if I continue to stay focused and determined. With positive people in my life like you, Dad, Sidnee and Kesia, I'll be damned to let myself fail."

And I believed him with all my heart.

TWELVE

The Penitentiary

On May 18, 2005, Marell phoned to let us know he had been moved to Pasquotank Correctional Institution in Elizabeth City, North Carolina. His tone was cut-and-dried as he explained that he was using another inmate's call time. It would take a few days before he could get on the call list. This was something new, maybe like the visitors' list at Harnett, only for stricter recordkeeping of phone calls.

Pasquotank was the same distance, almost to the exact mile, from my home as Foothills had been, but in totally the opposite direction. Now again, I would face the struggle of a four-hour drive each way, but instead of going into the mountains of North Carolina, I'd be heading towards the Outer Banks, practically to Virginia.

I had very bad feelings about Pasquotank even then, way before the recent violence when inmates killed four guards. I'd been locked into a theory about the place for years because if you are ever going to run into a person who has been in prison, it would be working at a recreation center. Many of the adults who came to the basketball free-play two evenings a week had been locked up at some point in their lives. Some of them had been inmates in Pasquotank, others had only heard about it through the system, and all of them had stories to tell.

Pasquotank was called one of the five worst prisons in the state. "Worst" meant to me that my son would be in danger at all times. The state's most dangerous inmates were sent there because prison authorities considered them a serious threat to the staff and other prisoners.

One good thing, though: Marell would be living alone in a cell that had a toilet and a sink. But he'd be shut in behind a sliding door that a guard at a station opened and closed electronically. He might be let out of his cell for one hour a day to exercise or shower. Even then, he'd be kept inside an armed perimeter of fences and guards who pointed guns. If he ever left the "pod," as they called it, he'd be in restraints and under armed supervision by COs. For the first time in my life, I really understood what "being under the gun" meant. In a maximum security prison, it's almost like being in the hole all the time, except that prisoners get to make calls and have visitors.

First thing Marell did was to complete the complicated paperwork required to use the phone. This would give some level of communication with us because, as his new caseworker explained, visits would not begin until June.

Waiting for Marell's first letter, I worried myself into a nervous frenzy. Nearly a week passed before his letter came. He began it by apologizing for taking so long to write. Having a cell to himself had enabled him to regroup and do some soul searching, but his tone was dark and withdrawn. It gave no comfort to me. Matter of fact, it made me feel like there was no bottom in my stomach.

I sensed that Marell felt shaky too. For the first time he used the word "penitentiary" in describing Pasquotank as a lot stricter than Harnett. He wrote about inmates who had messed up in other prisons and couldn't be handled anywhere else. Marell was my son, and I loved him no matter what his choices had been, but when I read his words, I thought, "Well, looky here, the pot calling the kettle black!"

At Pasquotank there would be no days of chilling in the yard. He'd be staying inside with "the worst of the worst," as he called them. Those men cared about no one and nothing, and it was common for him to see them stabbing each other with sharp objects. Extra time was meaningless to inmates with multiple life sentences. Marell vowed to avoid "the shady cats," even those from Fayetteville.

But it was hard for him to stay under the radar with the "homeboys." They weren't in formal gangs, but they were groups of inmates as hardcore as "Bloods" or "Crips," only without the titles. Inmates from Fayetteville automatically looked to each other in a fight and told Marell, "When we roll, you roll too." I'd written him a letter with tough talk about staying away from these guys, and once when he had a confrontation with one of them, he kept my words in mind and got away to his cell. If only he would have walked away from every fight.

Somehow the June days seemed to pass quickly, and we were soon travelling north on I-95 for our first visit to Pasquotank. James and I missed church that Sunday in order to make full use of our scheduled time with Marell.

We spoke very little during our drive, which seemed to take longer than it should have. This was a new area of travel for us, and we did not know what to expect. Once we left the interstate, there were no direct highways, and the roads were bad. We tried to enjoy the scenery, but nothing was beautiful, just long flat stretches with fewer and fewer communities. Then we saw only farmhouses with cows in fields. Finally, we made a turn into a long, long driveway that cut through the land surrounding the large correctional facility. It was enclosed by a razor wire fence and guarded by an armed patrol.

We found a place to park and entered the building where we checked in. First, we walked through a metal detector. I'd worn a belt that had some metal on it, so the machine beeped, and a female CO patted me down. I hated that procedure. The feel of the officer's hands on me was sickening.

When COs were sure we had no weapons, we were moved to a little hallway. We waited until we heard a buzzer, pulled on the door to open it, and proceeded on a sidewalk to the next building where there was a lobby as well as offices and restrooms. Then we were brought into a little chamber that held about eight to ten visitors. We heard doors banging and saw officers up ahead. None of the prison doors opened at the same time so that just a certain number of people could pass through a door at once. This process was nothing I'd never experienced before, but I realized it was one more way to prevent prisoners from becoming escapees.

The whole place gave me an eerie feeling. Eyes everywhere were watching us. While we waited to be escorted into another area, we looked up and saw the COs in a booth above us staring down from behind tinted windows. When time came to move ahead, James and I held back so that we could be sure to stay together. I felt like Dorothy, scared and anxious waiting for the Wizard of Oz to appear from behind the curtain. I did not know what to expect on the other side of those clanging prison doors, but I hoped that happiness would be there when I saw my son.

When we finally got to the visiting area, we saw several rows of tables each with about four chairs around them. These tables and chairs were so close together that we had to work to avoid bumping people as we squeezed past them to find a place for ourselves. Then we sat and waited until the sliding metal door clanged open. We couldn't see who was behind the door so we didn't know who was about to come out. One by one, a prisoner would emerge, and we and the other visitors would stand to see if it was our person. I was already on edge, and every time that door clanged opened or closed, I jumped.

After about ten minutes, Marell appeared. It was so good to see his smile again, even if this visit would be very different from the ones at Harnett. No inmates taking pictures here, no snacks bought through the canteen, and seats so close that we couldn't help hearing what other inmates and their visitors said, like we were all part of one big conversation.

I automatically greeted these people with "Hello" or "How are you today?" But Marell said, "Ma, you don't have to speak to them." This was his time to feel separate from that prison population and to be with us. And he wanted us to speak in low voices because he didn't think anyone needed to know our business.

Marell repeated what he'd written in his letters and said in phone calls: Pasquotank was "no joke." He asked again if we'd heard from Mr. Newsome, but there was nothing new to report. The attorney repeated over and over that he was waiting for the circumstances to be just right before he made a move.

After an hour had passed, we were struggling to have a conversation. Still, I dared not leave before the time was up, so James and I grabbed at things going on at home. But Marell was doing nothing in Pasquotank, so he had nothing to talk about. He knew there were things I didn't want him to talk about, and I knew there were things he never wanted me to ask. I was still curious about what his cell was like, who he lived near, what the bathrooms, dining hall, and food were like. I didn't have a picture in my mind of his surroundings, but that was a topic I didn't bring up again after our first visit at Polk. Marell had made clear then that he didn't want to discuss these things at all. Perhaps he thought certain details about his situation might upset me, but that left my imagination free to worry. Did he have a blanket on his cot if he was cold? For the first four years he was away, that thought had crept into my head at night and kept me from sleeping.

So between what Marell wouldn't discuss and what we didn't feel free to bring up, our silence with each other became noticeable. That would have been okay except that it was filled with chatter from other inmates and their visitors about things like a grandma in the hospital. Some people were arguing, and the noise level was miserable. Every once in a while, I'd sneak a glance at the other inmates. They made me uncomfortable, more so than inmates in the other prisons. I wondered what the guy to my left or to my right had done to get sent to Pasquotank.

Had other visitors heard the same stories we had heard about fights there? Stories about what a guard or a prisoner had done to someone? I realized that I saw Marell through a different pair of glasses. He was not like other inmates. He had been raised in a stable environment, with two parents and with rules and guidelines. So why were James and I sitting at this table with Marell amongst *those* inmates? Then I wondered, would other visitors be uncomfortable wondering what *my* son had done?

At that moment I realized Marell was no different than those inmates all around us. But I refused to allow myself to feel what I was thinking.

The next visit was two weeks later. Sidnee came with me instead of James, and that was the day she and I reached a silent understanding about Marell.

Sid was fourteen now, and when we pulled up to Pasquotank, she immediately noticed an armed CO riding around the parking lot with a gun drawn. She saw armed officers in the towers and the security truck circling the premises. I could see by her expression that she understood that if Marell was there, he had done something very wrong. She understood he was deep in trouble.

So we never had that conversation where we sat down together and I said, "Let me explain what happened." My intelligent child put things together herself. And over the following years, when her brother made more bad choices in prison, she'd say to him: "Enough is enough." She'd talk rough to him, just like we did.

But that summer day in Pasquotank, thanks to Sidnee, our visit was light-hearted and full of laughter. Marell joked with her the whole time, and I refrained from asking him anything serious. Time passed quickly without any silences. And when Sid and I walked through the doors to leave, tears ran down my face. I hugged her and told her that she had made her brother and me so happy.

Before we could visit Marell in Pasquotank again, he would be moved, a reminder—though I didn't really need one—that I had no control over his life, and neither did he.

THIRTEEN

The Dark Shadow

On July 20, 2005, I was relieved to learn that Marell had left Pasquotank, and I was downright happy when I realized that he'd be closer to home. Lanesboro Correctional Institution was in a poor, rural county less than a two-hour drive southwest of our home in Fayetteville. That prison had opened just a year and half before Marell arrived. It was new and clean, and I was sure he'd have enough heat in the winter. But I quickly saw that Lanesboro was every bit as bad as Pasquotank.

Lanesboro actually had the reputation for being one of the most corrupt, violent prisons in the state. It housed around 1,800 inmates, almost 1,000 of them in close custody, and like at Pasquotank, these men had committed two or three murders and were serving multiple life sentences. Lanesboro was so bad that in one year's time, six inmates killed themselves, and many other inmates deliberately hurt themselves, something that often happens when prisoners are held for a long time in solitary. Inmates also assaulted each other as well as the COs. The inmates even boasted to guards, "We'll let you go home today." The state's worst felons seemed to be running the place, and many of them were in gangs.

I wasn't naïve about the presence of gangs in Fayetteville. Even still, whenever there had been crime in my neighborhood, I never knew it to be gang-related. For my job at the rec center, I'd gone to conferences that enlightened me how to look out for signs of gang activity. And I'd heard about murders as part of initiations into gangs, like the one involving that white supremacist who had been in the Cumberland County Jail with Marell. Then there was a case of a young woman, an employee at Burger King, who had been abducted while she was closing up. She was put in the trunk of a car but escaped before being killed as part of a gang initiation.

For these reasons, I guess, I'd questioned whether Marell's involvement in Mr. Sawyer's murder had to do with gangs. But in Lanesboro, there were no questions about gangs. They were there, and they ruled.

Lanesboro was a dark shadow that hung over us for eighteen months. Looking back, I find it hard to remember details about when this or that happened. On the one hand, 2005 was a year that lingered. It seemed as if more than twelve months went by before we finally got to 2006. On the other hand, things happened fast and furious. Now, even re-reading Marell's letters, I don't see things clearly. My memory is blurry, and what I do remember doesn't always make sense to me.

But this I do know: Marell was in the hole-whether in Harnett, Pasquotank or Lanesboro-for half of 2005. "I'm still in the box" is how he'd begin his letters. He became more depressed than I'd ever seen him before. The matter of the drug charges was finally settled. And for the first time, gangs were a daily threat to his wellbeing.

By mid-September, Marell had been in Lanesboro barely two months when he received an A12 charge without any rights to appeal it. An A12 was given when an inmate was found to "manufacture, possess, introduce, sell or use any unauthorized controlled substance, unauthorized intoxicant or alcoholic beverage, or possess associated paraphernalia." I didn't know exactly what trouble sent Marell to the hole. Perhaps he'd been fermenting liquor out of fruit and sugar in his cell. Maybe he'd been caught with cigarettes that hadn't come from the canteen. Whatever he'd done, he'd be going to the hole, and when he got out, he would not be allowed to have contact visits for the following six months.

So it was not 'til late November that I finally laid eyes on him in Lanesboro. Our last visit had been that summer day five months before in Pasquotank. This was the longest period in my life that I'd gone without seeing my son.

The lobby of the visiting area had a nice picture display of the warden, the secretary of prisons, and the governor. These were like the pictures you'd see in a doctor's office of the smiling staff, their way of saying: "Trust us. This is a good place. We are here for you. We take pride in what we do." But I knew not to be impressed.

I'd visited Marell behind a glass partition while he was in the Cumberland County Jail, but this was our first non-contact visit since he'd gone to prison. I wasn't able to hug him then and for some time to come, but I was thankful to get any kind of visit and grateful that my mother could see Marell while she was with us for Thanksgiving. I would have hated for her to come this long way and not be able to see her grandson.

Sidnee came with us, and it wasn't a long visit. Even with her cheerful talk, we could tell Marell was uncomfortable. Maybe he didn't like visiting from behind the glass, or maybe he didn't like hearing about what I would be cooking for Thanksgiving dinner. Even when Marell was not in trouble or in lock-up, he got very depressed during the holidays. This was when his loneliness was the worst, and he missed home the most. Thanksgiving dinner in prison meant a sliced, canned turkey with cold, clumpy gravy, whereas he knew that we'd be home having a big dinner with all the homemade trimmings.

I always wanted him to call when all the family gathered for the holidays. Sometimes he did, sometimes he didn't. He wasn't always comforted by talking to us; that made him more aware he wasn't at home. In fact, phone calls often made him feel sadder.

Same with visits. When he wrote us during the first week of December, he was in the hole again receiving backlogged time carried over from Harnett. He said that instead of looking forward to seeing us, he became so depressed after visits that he wanted me to slow them down. He'd rather that we didn't come at all.

When it did bring him joy to have even non-contact visits, Marell worried that he'd show up looking rough. His CO seemed unable to locate his bag of personal hygiene items. He'd lost canteen privileges in the hole so he couldn't get his soap or the cologne he liked to use after shaving. That disappointed him because he always wanted to look and smell good for us at visits.

Marell was a neat freak, and while he was in Lanesboro, he swapped canteen items with another inmate for a newer pair of pants. The ones Marell had been issued were old and worn. He wanted clean and neat pants with a nice crease. He kept his tennis shoes clean too. Every day brought a different struggle to maintain the little dignities he'd grown up expecting.

For the first time, Marell talked about meals being skimpy, especially in the hole where he didn't have the snacks he could purchase from the canteen or win in card games. But even in the hole, inmates were allowed to receive a Christmas box, and James and I ordered one for him each year.

The goodies in a Christmas box came directly from a company under contract with the North Carolina Department of Correction. That company would provide inmates with a list of various candies, chips, beef jerkies, packaged beef and noodles, and other snacks. The inmate would check off what he wanted, then mail the list to whoever was going to pay for the box. That person then sent the list straight to the company along with a money order. The cost of each box could not be over $75.00. If the total on a list came to $75.06, you'd have to take something off in order to stay under the limit.

Every year Marell was in prison, he received a gift box. By itself, that wouldn't have been such a great expense, but there were so many others. Collect phone calls were as much as $5.00 or $6.00 for less than fifteen minutes when you subtracted the recorded messages from our time. The FCC passed a law in 2013 that calls from prison could not cost more than $3.75 (or $.25 a minute) for fifteen minutes, but by that time, our family had spent thousands of dollars on calls. The gas back and forth for each visit sometimes cost as little as $2.00 a gallon but often much more, so over the years, we spent thousands of dollars on gas in order to visit with Marell.

Then there was the money I'd put in his account so that Marell could have his necessary hygiene items as well as a few treats. This account allowed him to pay fees for other things, like doctor or dentist visits. Every two weeks, when I got paid, I'd take out a money order for around $40.00 to $45.00 and send it to the prison, where it would be deposited in Marell's account. He might use as much as $40.00 a week to pay for his necessities and snacks. When times were good in the Williams household—if I'd had an extra job taking pictures, for example—I might put more money in. When things were bad, it might be as little as $15.00. I treated Marell's prison account just like it was one of my regular bills, like the mortgage or water or light bill.

So when Christmas rolled around with all my extra holiday expenses, I was grateful that my mother and daddy, Aunt Rutha Mae, and others came through with a donation toward that $75.00 gift box. And I'll never forget the kindness of friends and family who would help us each month with the extra money they'd put in Marell's account.

Every day since I'd gotten that call from the Harnett County Jail, I worried: Would Marell get thirty more years on top of what he was already serving for those drug charges? On December 12, 2005, my question was answered.

James had to work that day, and I chose not to accept anyone's offer to ride with me to Harnett County Courthouse. I needed that forty-minute drive to think and pray alone. Even though I got up extra early, I could not get myself ready. No matter how confident the lawyer had been, no matter how much faith I had that God would direct our path, I was still afraid to hear the judge announce his decision.

James kept assuring me, as he did so many times, that things would work out. That was one of the days I forgot how much he was going through too, that he was worried and scared for Marell just like I was. But when James insisted, "It's time for Marell to own up to his bad choices and accept responsibility," his voice took a slightly louder tone like it always did when he was really serious. But then he spoke to me more softly: "I know it's hard for you, but we got to do it, Baby. It's for his own good, Baby."

By the time I left home, traffic was terrible. There was no chance that I would make it to the court by 9:00 a.m. I began breathing heavily, my stomach in knots. There was no one to hold my hand or hug me for comfort. It was just God and me, and I spoke aloud words of comfort from the book of Proverbs 3:5–6: "Trust in the Lord with all of your heart, and lean not on your own understanding. In all your ways acknowledge

Him. And He shall direct your paths." Within minutes, I received the calmness I needed.

I was late, yet I prayed that Marell's name had not been called before I made it to the second floor courtroom. When I entered, it was crowded, but I found a seat mid-way where I could view all angles. The judge was still calling the roll, and within fifteen minutes of leaving my car in the parking lot, I heard Marell's name.

He walked in, taking those little shuffling steps because his feet were chained together, and his hands were cuffed to each other. He seemed nervous as he looked around before his eyes finally found me in the courtroom.

Mr. Newsome whispered something to Marell, who nodded in response. Even though Marell had tried to bluff his way out of the drug charges, he finally understood that whether he knew what was in the bag or whether didn't know what was in the bag, he got caught with the bag, and he was guilty. So he had agreed to plead guilty on the three charges.

The attorney had always been confident that if he waited for the right judge at the right time, Marell would serve his sentences concurrently. Was this finally the right judge? And the right time?

Mr. Newsome began his opening statements. Marell had been caught up in a situation, he said, but now he was doing well in courses that would prepare him to adjust to life after prison, courses that coached him toward positive thinking and learning how to organize and plan, and to control his temper. Never mind that Marell had told me how boring these courses were; he had learned how to give the right answers and play the game.

Next Mr. Newsome told the judge that Marell's parents worked in the community, his father for Cumberland County Schools and his mother for the City of Fayetteville: "His father would be here right now, your honor, if he could have gotten the day off from work." Then the attorney turned and pointed at me, so that the judge could see that I was there for my son.

Mr. Newsome made this little spiel mechanically, with no particular emotion. Clearly he'd said this or something like this a hundred times before. Seemed like he knew how to play the game too.

The next words came from the judge, who surprised me when he blasted Marell: "Do you know how lucky you are to have parents who support you? How did you get involved in this terrible situation? You should be ashamed."

I was glad he said this. I hoped his words would help Marell, but by now, I had my doubts. He was a full adult. He'd been away from home for a long time. And I had to admit I'd seen him change.

Then the judge calmly reminded Marell of his plea and the possible punishment it could carry, and, reading from a paper in his hand, he sentenced my son. The time to be served for the drug charge would run concurrent with Marell's prior sentence for Mr. Sawyer's murder. Marell would not serve any additional time.

Before I realized what I was doing, I stood and sputtered: "God is good!" Immediately I composed myself and sat back down. With his attorney, Marell was quickly escorted out of courtroom through side doors. While he was walking out, he kept looking back at me and puckering his lips in a kiss in my direction. I never got a chance to speak to him before he went back to the prison in Lanesboro.

But I rushed down to the first floor in hopes that I could meet the attorney. I wanted to thank him and find out where we went from here, but I never eyed him. So I walked toward the door, when out of the blue, a woman came over and hugged me.

I didn't know this lady. She was white, probably middle aged, with dark hair, dressed in slacks. I guess she was being kind, but at first I was shocked that this stranger had her arms around me. Seeing my startled expression, she pushed away and asked:

"Was that your son in court?"

"Yes," I answered, still wondering who she was and why she wanted to know.

"You are a strong mother." She leaned in and whispered, "God has your back." That was it. She walked back toward the elevator as if she was heading back to court. I never learned her name and never saw her again.

The woman's words gave me peace during my ride back to Fayetteville. I'd driven to the court thinking there would be no one to comfort me, but this complete stranger had come from out of nowhere with a hug and kind words. And I remembered another white lady—that CO I had talked to in the courthouse ladies' room the day of Marell's first appearance on the drug charges. She had also comforted me with her politeness and concern.

And I think about the judge who said, "May God be with you" when Marell made his first court appearance way back in February of 1996, and the detective who allowed Marell to come home that horrible morning after he had confessed. Regardless of what the police had planned that day, whatever their true motives for bringing Marell home, they put me in a place where I got to pray with my son. I cannot count all the times someone showed me kindness when I did not expect it. Not only my family and church members, but officials who spoke courteously when I called to inquire about something for Marell—so many people showed that they understood I was just a mother worried about her son.

So that stranger at the Harnett County Courthouse was surely one of God's markers on a long, rough road to let me know I was headed in the right direction. She and others were evidence that He walked with me: "For I know the thoughts that I think toward you, says the Lord, thoughts of peace and not of evil, to give you a future and a hope." These words from Jeremiah 29:11 were my strength.

Being the mother of an inmate seemed to control my life, but other personal relationships were brewing.

First off, there was James. One of the great blessings of my life is that we stayed solid. People ask me how we managed through hard times when so many marriages crash under the strain of a son's problems. I answer, "We had God in our lives."

James and I had started out with a good friendship. He was and is still my best friend. He was always patient, understanding, and considerate, even when I know I was difficult to deal with.

We sometimes differed about how to be the parents of an inmate, especially when it came to visiting Marell. Whenever there was a chance, I went. Good thing James is a workaholic because he was busy with his lawn care business on weekends; he always wanted to provide the best he could for us. So we wouldn't have spent every weekend together anyway, but many times he wanted me to stay home. "Rosalind, you can't do this. You keep going every weekend," he'd say. "You have no break." He worried about me and my health.

He also worried about the money I was spending on gas when we were barely making it to the next paycheck. Sometimes James would flat out say, "There's not enough money to travel to visit Marell this weekend." Then I would postpone paying a credit card bill and take a late fee or borrow money or cash a check I'd gotten for a birthday present in order to make the trip.

"There is no changing your mind when it comes to Marell," James would say, and I'd say back, "You're the man in my life." Then James would answer gently and softy, "Yes, me and Marell." I hated when my husband said that sort of thing, and now I wonder exactly how much it did bother him. We had that conversation many times, and it made me determined to let him know how much I appreciated him. He was my biggest support, the person I could always lean on.

As long as we've been married, we insisted on making time for ourselves. So I juggled my responsibilities to make sure that continued. James and I would take little vacations, even if only for an overnight trip. We'd even accept invitations from developers to look at resort properties just to get a free couple of days at the beach.

I always wanted to do something special or different when our anniversary rolled around. I might string cutout hearts or the words "Happy Anniversary" on the wall of the hall to our bedroom. James and I always posed for anniversary pictures together. When we did that, we knew we had to hold one another and smile, and if we smiled and put our arms around each other, we took ourselves to a happy place. Even in the midst of the roughest times, we made a reason to smile.

James always loved my cooking, especially my sweet potato and apple pies. Making them was a thank-you to him. Family meals were, and still are, sacred in our home. Any time we sit down to eat, even if it is only to have a snack, we offer up thanks. Even on our worst days, James and I found something to thank the Lord for together. Another thing we did daily, we'd greet each other and say goodbye with an automatic kiss. James starting doing that when we got married and still does that today. That's how we stayed strong together.

But the finger that I pressed on my children was getting weak. My influence on all three had been scattered. I wasn't part of the hustle-bustle of the girls' lives any more. I was seeing less of them. Kesia focused on studying for the North Carolina Bar exam so that she could start her career. Like many other graduates from law school, she was working at various jobs to pay her bills and law school debt. Other things took precedence over coming home and joining me to visit her brother. And Sidnee also now felt free to decline coming with me sometimes, even though she knew her brother would be disappointed. I understood it was her choice to make. She was growing up, spending less time with me too. She warned me that in another year, she might not accompany me on visits at all. I laughed, but I understood. She was fifteen and growing up.

But I did not have the privilege of staying home. Visiting Marell was part of my second job. Even still, Marell seemed to have slipped away. He was the center of his own world where everyone owed him something. If something was not going in his favor, he acted like someone better snap to and make it right. Prison makes some men selfish, especially if the prisoner has a family ready to make sacrifices, visit him, deposit money in his account, and call lawyers and prison officials whenever anything might be done to make his life better. We were always giving, giving, giving, and he came to expect that we always had it to give. "I know you don't have the money for a pizza," he'd say, and then he'd ask for a pizza. Nine times out of ten, I'd make it happen by putting extra money in his account so that he could draw on it for a special meal.

There had been a time when I might have had influence over Marell's behavior. Not now. Among the many things that I will never understand is how we still hoped that he could get out of prison in 2012. Even with his sentence for the drug charges running concurrently, no math explains how 2012 was the year he could be released, if only he stayed clear of trouble.

So you'd think that knowing he'd dodged a big bullet with those drug charges, he'd say to himself: "I'm so thankful to God, and the judge, and my momma and family and the lawyer for helping me. I could have spent the rest of my life in prison, but I can still get out in seven years. I'm more than half way through my time. I will stay out of trouble."

But that didn't happen. This was Marell's season to be involved in violence. His behavior made me upset and mad and disappointed. Still, I had to wonder. Could anyone stay out of trouble in a place like Lanesboro? It was either fight or become a victim.

"Ma, you can't help but get in trouble. I've got to maintain in here," he'd say. When fights got stirred up, he'd make it seem like he tried to walk away, but then he had no choice except to get personally involved. I was a mother who loved her son, and he loved me, I'm sure. But my love got in the way, got me swooped up by his manipulation. He'd tell me what I wanted to hear, and he always had an excuse for it, even if *it* was something we'd discussed staying away from.

After a while, even when he was adamant about his innocence in certain incidents, I'd think, "Well whoop-di-do! This time you're innocent? Other times you couldn't help it? Other times you're guilty?" How was I supposed to pick and choose?

Marell could see the change in me. For years I had patiently listened to whatever he had to say, but I'd learned that things didn't change for the better by patiently listening. I was tired of his crap. I was always on edge, waiting for the next phone call with bad news. And it came in a way I never expected.

Marell had adopted a no-fear, cocky attitude that pissed Kesia off. Neither of them was bashful with expressions *about* the other *to* the other. This became apparent when Marell called the house one weekend while Kesia was at home. She accepted his collect phone call and their conversation quickly led to an argument over a little nothing, something minute. It was Marell's tone that got to her.

I heard only Kesia's side: "You're not going to talk to me that way!" But when I overheard her say, "You don't scare me," I realized he was trying to bully her. I grabbed the phone, and he accused me of taking up for his sister. After I hung up, Kesia said that Marell had cursed at her and that I was taking *his* side.

I was boiling. These were *my children* disrespecting each other and putting me in the middle.

Some days after this ugly phone call, Kesia received a letter from Marell. If I was looking for an apology in it, I was dead wrong. He was still angry. He expected Kesia to give him the kind of "respect" that he had somehow obtained in prison. And then there were his threats ("when I get out, you're going to see," that sort of thing). To his own sister!

A mother's pain when her children are feuding shakes her heartbeat. Kesia was hurt, and I was too. She wanted answers and looked to me with accusations. "He can talk to me that way, and you have nothing to say!" she shouted.

This was the worst confrontation Kesia had with Marell since he'd gone away, but it was like so many others where Kesia felt I did nothing to bring Marell in line and she got the brunt of any disciplining. Sure, I could reprimand my son and scorn his behavior, but my daughter saw this as just a tap on the wrist. I couldn't spank him or punish him like I did when they were younger. I had no control over him. Kesia must have realized that, yet she still expected me to make things right.

But that letter from Marell forced me to take action. I mentioned my plans to no one, and to this day I haven't told Kesia what I did. I immediately scheduled an appointment to visit Marell. This was going to be a difficult conversation, and I cried during my entire drive to Lanesboro. When I got there, I was so preoccupied with what was coming that for the first time, the misery of the check-in process didn't sink in.

Marell was out of the hole, so this would be one of our few contact visits in Lanesboro and the first visit with him since his letter to Kesia. When he entered the visiting room, his expression told me he feared what I was there to say.

I wasted no time. I told him that I would be the one doing the talking, and I kept my voice low, stern, and persuasive. "I don't care what kinda power you have in here, but it means nothing to me. You have changed. You seem heartless. You have become a son that I do not know and do not want to know."

Had it come to this? I couldn't believe those words were coming out of my mouth. I had been shocked when a woman told me she was done with her son who kept messing up in prison. She wasn't going to see him or even put money in his account any more. When she told me that, I thought, how could a mother be like that?

Half standing, I got up and wagged my finger in Marell's face.

"You and Kesia both came out of my womb. I will not allow either to disrespect the other in this lifetime. What one of you does to the other affects me too. Where is the Marell that I raised? Until he is ready to return, do not call or write me."

For the first time in a long time, I witnessed tears in Marell's eyes. I got up and left. The visit took exactly twenty-one minutes. Four hours of driving for a twenty-one minute visit. Even though it was long drive for a very short visit, I had spoken my mind truthfully and felt some relief.

In a few days, Marell called to apologize, but it would take more than a conversation to mend our feelings and more time still for Kesia to reconcile with her brother.

In March of 2006 I got a phone call that Uncle Junior had been killed in a terrible two-car accident. He had died at the scene. The family was in shock, and I had to find a way to tell Marell.

I called the prison and spoke with an officer. "My son is an inmate at Lanesboro Correctional," I said, "and we need to tell him that his uncle has died." The CO assured me that Marell would be called into a private area, something that happened from time to time when a caseworker wanted to speak to an inmate, so he wouldn't necessarily suspect that he was going to hear bad news. But this would be different because that day there would be a chaplain waiting for him, and he'd tell Marell about

Uncle Junior. Marell would then be allowed to stay in the room to grieve privately and to call home.

When Marell did call us, his voice was weary, and he was sniffling back his tears. The death of Uncle Junior hit Marell in a very deep place. I knew that he would have to keep his emotions bottled up. Where would he go when he needed to cry? How many times had I run to my bedroom at home or to the bathroom at work to shed my tears in private? But Marell had no private place where he could break down. Even though he needed to cry like a baby, he had to maintain his prison tough-man image. I worried that Marell would act his grief out in anger. He could easily go off if another prisoner or guard confronted him. No one was going to give him the benefit of the doubt, understanding that this was his sad time.

To add to Marell's misery, he was worried about me and the rest of the family; we were all suffering from our loss. He wanted to be with us at the funeral services and the family gatherings, but that was not allowed. There was no Major Whirley at Lanesboro to bend the rules a little. So not only had Marell lost his loved one, he had lost his opportunity to grieve and heal with family members. Who would he have in prison to hold him or give him a shoulder to cry on? He was alone.

Then I thought about other prisoners when they were grieving. How did they adapt, always being on alert and proving themselves even during sad, fearful, and lonesome times? Grief surely created more stress, instability, and trouble in a prison.

So I knew I had to keep in constant communication with Marell, to remind him that this too shall pass. The sun would shine again and soon! I welcomed him to call if he needed to talk or express anything.

In our time of sorrow, I realized I'm not a person to hold grudges. I could never be like that woman who said she was done with her son. Marell was *my* son. He apologized for what he'd said to Kesia, and I saw the change in him, at least in the visits and the calls. I was eager to move forward.

Pretty soon, Marell entered a new phase in his prison life that took his mind off his tribulations. He befriended an inmate-I'll call him John-who was working on getting his sentence reduced. That he had a "friend" was a new development, a change from his earlier time in prison when he said, "Ma, there are no friends here, only acquaintances."

John had been able to get his case taken back to court. He hoped for a reduction in his sentence and hyped Marell up regarding his own case. Getting his sentence reduced became Marell's conversation piece during every phone call and visit for several months.

By late September of 2006, he was showing energy and excitement that I had not observed since he'd taken those business courses when he was at Harnett Correctional. He sent me articles and learned everything he could about the law relating to his case. Together with John, Marell worked hard on each angle. He sent me a copy of a letter that he was going to present to the North Carolina Prisoner Legal Services which existed to aid prisoners who felt that they were wrongly found guilty or wrongly sentenced.

"Okay, sounds good," I said. I listened and let Marell talk, but I was torn. I was glad he was feeling upbeat again. If he could keep his mind on this sentence reduction, he might keep his mind off other things that got him in trouble.

But he was too confident. He was sure he was going to succeed. I was not. Matter of fact, his efforts shone a spotlight on him that he did not need. After talking with my friend who was an attorney, I tried to persuade Marell to let it go. He had no grounds to obtain a lesser sentence. His plea bargains were closed and over.

Still, Marell refused to give up, and now he was rallying advice from another "friend," another inmate who had managed to have his sentence reduced. Ryan came on board at that time, and Marell announced that they had common interests beyond their life in prison. They planned to become "business partners" after they got out, and he talked and talked about details for the business that they would start.

I had been sad when Marell had no one to lean on in prison, but I can't say that I was happy knowing he considered certain inmates his "friends." I feared that these friendships were not stable; they had no foundation other than that these men were in prison together. I wanted to say to Marell (but I didn't), "Here you are, the two of you in prison. How realistic is this business you're planning together?" But Marell was not held back by reality. The longer he stayed in prison, the less equipped he was to understand how life was outside. He just couldn't see beyond the prison walls.

Same for getting his sentence reduced. I knew he didn't have a chance, but Marell and John kept working on it. Marell even included him in our phone conversations so John could explain directly to me how his own sentence had been decreased. Marell believed if John had his sentence reduced, he could too. But their situations were very different; they were in for very different crimes. Marell ignored those facts.

For the next few months, Marell kept busy sending letters to law clerks and his public defenders, Vernon Stevenson and Timothy Drake, as well as to Judge Lee Cramer. Marell didn't claim he'd been poorly represented or that he wanted to change his plea agreement. His point was that he had been sentenced for a "total" of 196 months, yet according to the judgment from office of the clerk of court (which I obtained for Marell) his sentence was for 245 months. Marell claimed that he had not received a "minimum or maximum corresponding sentence" and cited North Carolina General Statutes, 15A-1420 (d) in one letter and 15A-1340

17(e) in another. He quoted the dictionary definition of "total" and used legal terms like "sua sponte."

Responses to his letters trickled in until January 2007, and all of them basically said, "Are you serious?" I could imagine Mr. Stevenson laughing when he wrote, "I do not think your scheme has any chance whatsoever of succeeding." The North Carolina Prisoner Legal Services laid it out. Marell had no options unless he withdrew his guilty plea and went back to court. A new trial and a jury might find him guilty of first-degree murder and sentence him to life in prison. In fact, that had just happened to another inmate who had withdrawn a guilty plea. He got a new trial and a new sentence twice as long as the first.

Marell still wouldn't give up. He kept telling me to make calls and write letters on his behalf. Finally, I just had to say, "No." No more calls. No more letters. I knew it was futile. I was tired, and the idea of Marell's resentencing had become a weight on me.

So his discussion of a possible resentencing faded, at least in our letters and conversations. Perhaps Marell persisted without telling his family. But somehow the matter of resentencing went away. I never mentioned it again, and I was grateful that this disappointment didn't seem to hit him hard.

One problem disappeared, but another much bigger one surfaced.

Marell wrote us that he was "under investigation." He was in the hole, this time because *someone* had written a letter to a prison official accusing him of *something*. The COs didn't show Marell the letter or tell him who that someone or what that something was.

I wondered, could it be the card games Marell put together where inmates gambled for canteen items? Gambling and contraband were strictly against the rules, so of course I was terribly worried about this. Here again, there was nothing I could do but give my opinion, and he'd just respond, "Ma, everybody does it."

Then I reasoned with myself: "This stuff with the cards is bad, but it could be worse." Perhaps that's how the COs felt because they seemed to let it slide. After all, Marell had been running card games since he was at Harnett Correctional, and he'd never gotten in trouble for it. Until now?

I was always aware that Marell could finagle and word things so that you'd believe him. But after a bit, he convinced me that he was in the hole only because some inmate on the block just wanted him gone.

One thing going for Marell was that he was blessed to have a caseworker who went to bat for him. Mr. McNair was one of the good ones who did his job carefully. Marell liked the man because he didn't let papers sit on his desk for weeks waiting for a response. He got things done promptly and kept track of Marell's points for good behavior which would get him moved to a minimum custody facility. Not every caseworker kept up with details the way Mr. McNair did, so Marell was confident that he'd be in the hole only a few days. And that's exactly what happened.

Early in January of 2007, Sidnee and I visited Marell prior his thirtieth birthday. This was another of those bittersweet occasions. My son was turning thirty. Though we couldn't bring him a cake or presents, at least we had a face-to-face visit, and I could give him a big hug.

We talked about his self-help courses and how they could get him transferred to a medium custody facility closer to home. He was optimistic and swooped me up into his hopes. After all, back when he'd been at Foothills, he'd been at the bottom of a long list to be transferred, and then-boom! He was sent to Harnett. So getting to a minimum custody facility wasn't one of his unrealistic schemes; he had a plan.

But things change at the drop of a hat. By his birthday on January 14th, he was back in the hole. Someone (same person as before? probably, but he didn't know) had written another letter to the administration, this time accusing Marell of planning an assault on an officer. It seemed to us that when the accusation in the first letter didn't stick, the writer went for something much bigger. This was a very serious accusation that could result in an A99 charge, years added to his sentence, more time in maximum, and months in the hole.

This "someone" was blatantly lying, Marell stated. This accusation fired him up tremendously. He knew what would happen if these charges stuck. He wrote about flipping out and really giving the COs a reason to keep him in the hole. Marell was depressed for real, and scared.

I should have been scared too, just as I had been when he got the drug charges. The charge of planning an assault on a CO could also keep him in prison for life. But I wasn't scared because I'd gone numb. I'd been through this kind of thing so often, I didn't feel fear like I used to. Marell was making his own choices, and I was letting go of my need to control.

Still, I did as he requested, and I called a prison official to find out if anything had been decided. I learned that Marell had not been officially charged with anything yet, but what the captain said made me sick to my stomach: Marell's charges might be gang affiliated, and Marell had been linked to gangs while in Pasquotank.

This prison official was very particular with the words he used, and I believed that he had given me information to connect some dots. I concluded that Marell had been abruptly moved out of Pasquotank to shut down tensions between one group and another.

But this phone conversation increased my suspicions that Marell could have been involved with gangs, maybe for years. I recalled different things that could fit that theory. He liked to wear red, and red was the color of the Bloods. But ever since middle school, Marell loved to wear red. He loved to see me in red. We sometimes took our family pictures with each of us wearing red shirts. I realized that I was only grabbing at straws. Just because he liked a certain color didn't give me real evidence that he had been in a particular gang back then.

Still, I couldn't stop wondering. Was he in a gang now? I'd lecture him on how being in a prison gang might affect him after he got out, how it might affect us. Would we be safe in our home if word on the street connected our son to a gang? I'd tell Marell, "Whatever goes on in prison will follow you when you get out." I even point blank asked, "Are you in a gang?" Never answering directly, yet never denying, he said back, "I have a lot of people I associate with."

A person's values change when he's in prison. Marell surely knew it would comfort me to deny that he was in a gang, but he might have felt more secure in prison by giving off the attitude that he was a gang member. Bottom line, I never really knew.

Writing about this now, I see that he wasn't the only one whose values had changed. I didn't want him to be in a gang, but I did want an explanation for the crime he'd committed, for the charges he got in prison, for going to the hole so often, and for getting in trouble so much-even if the explanation was something I hoped was not true. What I've written seems a little crazy.

The really crazy thing is, the rumors that Marell might be charged with planning to assault a guard just went away. The prison official's words had caused me think that a bubble was about to burst, but it never did. And after Marell served a few weeks in the hole, he was moved to the other side of North Carolina.

FOURTEEN
Still Standing

Lanesboro had drained my energy and had worn Marell out too. The constant trouble, gang accusations, and letdown after not getting resentenced had put him in a dark place. Returning to Lanesboro, even in memory, has put me under that cloud again. Now I'm finally out from under it. I'm relieved to start writing about my visits to a smaller facility called Maury Correctional. That's where Marell was from February 14, 2007, to June 21st of that year.

Maury housed more than a thousand medium and close custody inmates in different units. Prisoners with mental health issues, chronic illnesses, and veterans were put in separate buildings. Marell was in the regular population and that meant he could eventually participate in work assignments or programs that assisted inmates to reintegrate into the community after their release. I looked at Maury as a fresh start for Marell. He lay low there, passing his calmest months in a long time.

He was also in Maury for only four months, so my memory of the place is very vague, probably because I visited just a few times. I do recall it had opened a few months before Marell arrived, so it was new, but nothing to get excited about. When you've seen one prison, you've seen them all. They're just in a different town. And the ride to get there is different too.

Maury was two hours northeast of Fayetteville, and during my drive, I played my music to make the trip seem faster. Highway 70 cut through the rinky-dink country towns of Snow Hill and Farmville and through winding back roads that included miles and miles of farmland.

For whatever reason, my first visit took place on a weekday when school was in session. At one point during my drive, a school bus stopped in front of me to let children off. While I waited behind that bus, I gazed at the surroundings and noticed a beat up, broken-down barn to my right. This structure was in a field near a row of houses. The children getting off the bus walked toward them; they were livable and up-to-date. But the barn had a wall that looked like it had been punched in and was leaning to meet the opposite side. Its faded red front door hung by one hinge. If the wind blew, I just knew the door would swing right off. Grass had grown tall, covering a side window of the barn, and thin trees leaned on the back of it.

"That's my life," I thought. "Like that barn, I've been through many storms, taken the rain and wind, and I still stand. Just like that barn. Wow! I still stand!" After all the years of visiting Marell, with encouragement from others and faith in God, I was still standing.

Then I pulled out my camera (I take it everywhere) and snapped a picture.

I don't remember anything about my actual visit with Marell that day, but heading back home, I stopped and took more pictures of old barns. Taking those pictures excited me. I spent the rest of the ride home thinking I could make them into puzzles, and each one would represent my life as one of those beat up barns.

From then on, throughout Marell's prison time, I would stop either before or after a visit to take pictures. I was always tense when I was approaching a prison. Looking at the barns and photographing them and taking other pictures calmed me. This didn't make visits less painful, but I became more relaxed.

I never did anything with these pictures of barns besides sticking them in a folder. I wanted to use them to describe my life in some way. I still declare I will do that. And really, I am doing that now by using them to describe myself during the long ordeal of my son's imprisonment.

FIFTEEN

Illness and Death

On June 21, 2007, Marell landed in Hoke County Correctional.

I was already familiar with this facility because that's where a dear friend had served time. He had been housed at the hospital unit there after a serious injury. In fact, this prison had been built on the site of a hospital, the McCain Sanitarium, a place for people with tuberculosis back in the 1920s. In the 1950s, it was turned into a prison that housed around 500 men, most of them in minimum security, the others in medium.

Because I'd known that Hoke was supposed to have good medical facilities, I questioned Marell about his health. When he was in Lanesboro, he'd been diagnosed with high blood pressure and started on medicines. But he did not take this condition seriously. I'd thought little of high blood pressure, too, when I was thirty, even though I had family members with it. Then I got it at age forty and knew it could be a "silent killer." Every now and then, whether talking with Marell on the phone or during a visit, I'd remind him of that, but he'd say to me, "Ma, you're afraid of everything."

When it came to his health, this attitude was nothing new. From the time he was a child, he did not like going to a doctor or taking medicine. When he was in prison, it was the same. If I'd notice he had a cough, for example, I'd tell him to go to the doctor. But he didn't want to spend the $10.00 out of his account to pay for the appointment. That was Marell.

At least I could keep a closer eye on him at Hoke Correctional because the prison was located just a little more than twenty-nine miles from home. Being moved closer to us was one of the privileges that come when a prisoner starts to approach the end of his sentence. That way he can see more of his family and eventually begin supervised home visits.

Even with traffic, Hoke was only a forty-five minute drive that I was familiar with and looked forward to. Plank Road went right through Fort Bragg and was surrounded on both sides by woods where soldiers trained. Many times the road would be clogged with army trucks or training trailers that prevented me from passing. And right off Plank Road, as soon as you left Fort Bragg, there was Hoke Correctional.

The place reminded me of a fenced-in college dormitory. Even the COs referred to dorms instead of cellblocks. Rolls of barbed wire surrounded the place, and an officer stood watch from the tower. Still, the guards seemed friendly and relaxed, and getting in was less of an ordeal here than at the maximum security prisons like Pasquotank or Lanesboro. All we had to do was show ID and pass through metal detectors. It had been years since I'd experienced this kind of setup.

For the first time in a while, we were able to take pictures during visits. Because Marell was so close to Fayetteville, he got many visitors. My sister Andrea also traveled from Texas to see him with her kids, and they had two visits, which made Marell really happy. What made me happy was that he had a different, better attitude now. He was at ease. He'd stopped being a tough guy toward us and showed appreciation that family and friends could come back into his life.

In November my mother came for a week and a half, though she was able to have only one visit with Marell. Before she returned to Texas, we celebrated her birthday. I had cooked a big dinner and baked a cake. The whole family had gathered around to sing Happy Birthday while Mother and Marell were on the phone. Marell also got the chance to speak to Uncle Felton. It was a happy time.

Little did I know that I would soon make that nervous call again to a prison to tell Marell we had a death in the family. Uncle Felton had a major heart attack and passed. Marell seemed to take this news worse than Uncle Junior's death, maybe because he had spoken to Uncle Felton the evening before he died.

Marell inquired about coming to the service. He thought that being closer to home, it would be likely that he could, but he didn't think about all the logistics that were involved. He had been in jail when my grandmother passed, and Uncle Junior had paid the costs of getting Marell to her funeral. Now Uncle Junior was dead, and Marell was in prison. I had no idea what the costs would be for the mandatory guards to escort him back and forth, but I was sure that was something we couldn't afford. I also knew because Uncle Felton was not immediate family, according to how the prison figured it, the request would be denied. Marell argued that because his uncle babysat for him so much when he was little and had really helped me raise my children, Uncle Felton *was* immediate family. But I understood how the system would work on this, so I steered Marell away from the idea, and he sadly abandoned the thought. During our next visit, Marell was quiet as he viewed the pictures I brought from Uncle Felton's service.

Marell talked about the many programs available at Hoke and how he planned to take advantage of them. He even got a job cleaning. I thought he wouldn't like doing that kind of work, but he said he enjoyed getting out of his cell to clean the library and the computer room in the evenings. This also made me happy because I felt work would occupy his time and keep him busy and out of trouble.

But Marell could always take an opportunity and turn it into a worry. When he went into different rooms to clean, he would get on the computers and use the Internet. I learned about this not through him, but through people in Fayetteville who mentioned contacting him online.

I was furious. I dared not talk to him about it on the phone for fear that a prison official was listening in. So I waited 'til a visit when I warned him that he was pushing his luck, especially if he was contacting his friends through email. I never asked how he accessed the Internet, whether someone gave him a password or what. I didn't want to know how he did it. I just wanted it to stop. But it didn't.

The Internet was not Marell's only way of communicating with the outside world. Before leaving Lanesboro he had called me one time on a cell phone that he said he got from another prisoner. My first reaction was worry that the prison could trace his call back to me. Marell proclaimed there was no way to connect me to him with a pre-paid phone. Cell phones were the going thing around prison, he said. But I told him, "If you want to use a cell phone, it's on you. Do not call me on it again." He would have to call me collect through the prison phone or there would be no communication between us.

He didn't call me again from Lanesboro on that cell phone, but he got another one when he went to Hoke. Even though he never called home on his cell, I'd bump into different people around town who told me they talked to him at times when he wouldn't have been able to use the prison phone. I never questioned them or Marell about this. I didn't want to know anything about it or be part of it in any way.

I won't deny that I would have loved being able to talk to him at any time of night or day. But I refused this opportunity because I knew it wasn't right and could result in Marell having time added to his sentence, or good time taken away, or worse. That thought scared the crap out of me. The only way he could keep his medium status was if he stopped breaking the rules. I constantly told him to think about the consequences of his actions. I meant that, just as I'd meant all the advice I'd given him before. But more and more, I saw Marell lived for the moment, without fear for what could happen in the future.

Marell would be at Hoke Correctional for only six months, but during that time he briefly became excited about a new venture. "It's positive, Ma!" he said, and he wanted me to be involved in it.

One of the other prisoners had invited him to join a social group. He was flattered because not everyone got the invite, so he showed great interest in a group run by prisoners proclaiming the Islamic faith. I am not down on anyone's religion, but I was raised in the Church of Christ where Marell was raised too. Still, I accepted that Marell was grown and could make his own choices about religion. And really, I never seriously thought he'd convert to Islam. Before I could express any of this, Marell went quickly for some explanations and showed me that his interest in this group was purely for self-reward.

"Ma, I am not going to join that faith," he assured me. He'd gone to a couple of meetings where there was no message preached or study of the Islamic religion. According to Marell, members taught positive behavior to make people better so that they could empower the next human being. And the thing that Marell really liked, the prison allowed them to have monthly dinners with their families.

This would be a first. All the while Marell had been in prison, we'd never had a dinner where we could sit down and eat together. But now I could cook up food for a fellowship meeting that would take place at the prison with the inmates and their families. So I started preparing covered dishes, enough for at least eight to ten people.

But a few days before that dinner was to take place, the administration gave a vague reason for cancelling the event. I wasn't upset about this, but Marell got hot and fussed for a few days, expressing to the staff that they had disrespected me because I had already started cooking. He couldn't stand it when he thought I'd been inconvenienced or disrespected by someone else, though he didn't apply that thinking in other areas of his life, like how *his* behavior and choices had affected me.

After he finally calmed down, I never again heard him say anything about going to meetings with the Muslims.

SIXTEEN
Secrets

Before I knew it, Marell was back in Polkton, North Carolina, but thankfully not at Lanesboro Correctional. Matter of fact, many times when I had visited him at Lanesboro, I had noticed the entry to another prison across the road and on top of a hill. That's where Marell was sent on January 10, 2008, to Brown Creek Correctional, an older, medium/minimum security facility.

Since Sidnee and I knew how to get there, we arrived early, about thirty minutes before our first visit. When we saw how many people were already lined up to go through the security check, we got out of the car immediately and joined the line. While we waited, Sidnee noticed the stairs that led into the visitation area. From the outside, Brown Creek looked smaller than it really was, and she worried if I would be able to walk the distance and down all those steps.

Sidnee knew something I'd been keeping from Marell. On and off for ten years, I'd had health problems that had become very serious. Soon I would require surgery. Because I didn't want to worry my son, I hadn't told him about it and kept going to visits, never missing one because of my health.

I was able to manage the steps that day in Brown Creek, though I had to take my time, even with Sidnee's help. Because construction was going on in one of the dorms and it was a nice winter day, our visit was outside. According to Department of Correction rules, the temperature has to be sixty degrees or above for visits to take place outside.

Marell showed some anxiety during this visit, questioning why they brought him to Brown Creek. It was not close to home, and no photographs were allowed during visits. So it did feel like we were taking a step backwards by losing privileges that came when a prisoner is at a lower level of custody.

Looking back, I have my own theories about why Marell was moved out of Hoke after six months, and why before that he'd been moved out of Maury after four months, and why he would be moved from Brown Creek very soon. On and off I'd hear rumblings about gangs, though no one ever gave me any proof. I knew that the guards taunted Marell about being in a gang. And Marell would say things like "the gangs fought last night." He may have been observing, or maybe more, I didn't press to know.

I'm not saying that Marell had suddenly become a sweet innocent child who was sitting around quietly, but it had been a long time since he had been written up for fighting or infractions, at least nothing that got him into such trouble that I had heard about it or remember now. He hadn't been in the hole for more than a year, since he'd left Lanesboro in February of 2007. And he'd been keeping track of the points he earned for days of good behavior. He made progress toward minimum and never was sent back to a maximum security facility. So I wondered, did prison officials want to get him away from certain people, both guards and prisoners? Maybe somebody at the prison was looking out for Marell and thought he would stay out of trouble if he kept on the move? And, of course I did believe that Somebody was looking out for my son, and that Somebody was God.

Soon after my first visit to Brown Creek, Marell called to tell us "good news." He had a job on the road crew, picking up trash from the highways. I dared not question his excitement about a job that was nasty, hot, sweaty, smelly, and hard. He did not see it like that. He saw only the opportunity to be outside the prison walls and in a different world.

During my last visit to Brown Creek, Marell did say how tired he got working in the sun. He also described some fancy rims that he had seen on a car as it passed him on the highway, and that sparked a conversation about cars. When he got out, he said, he wanted a 70s Cadillac with rims like the ones he had seen. This happy-go-lucky story about what he'd have after prison showed me his priorities. I wanted to know, "What about getting a job to have the money to pay for these things?" But I kept quiet. When you are not privileged to see fancy rims on cars every day, I guess daydreaming about them makes time go by faster. So I began to understand why he liked the job picking up highway trash, and I recognized once again all the things in life that I took for granted.

Right before our visit ended that day, I was forced to explain to Marell that I would be unable to visit him for six to eight weeks because I was going to have surgery. He had fifty-one questions that I assured him I could answer when he called home. When he did phone, he had even more questions and worried about who was going to take care of me while I was recuperating. I insisted that I would be fine; my mother would come to help. I worried less about Marell, knowing that my mother would visit him with Sidnee or James. Marell would be okay, I told myself.

All these years later, I realize that if I thought he might worry about what was going on at home—like if someone was sick or my surgery coming up—I kept it from him. And he knew what would worry me. He never described how his cell or dorm looked, so I never could picture these places or him inside them. If he was involved with gangs, he never told me. He and I, we kept our secrets. There were things he didn't know about me and things I didn't know about him. We wanted to be protective of each other.

SEVENTEEN
Sunday Dinners

On June 19, 2008, about six weeks after my surgery, I was healing but weak when the phone rang. I picked up the receiver and heard an automated voice: "You have a collect call from Robeson County Correctional Center." Next thing I heard was Marell saying his name. He had been transferred to a minimum security facility just thirty-three miles away. To me, that was at our back door.

That prison had been built in the 1930s, and it was small, with around 300 inmates. The men slept in dormitories with double bunk beds and used group toilets and showers. But only one fence surrounded the place. There was no watchtower with armed guards. Even though the dormitories were routinely patrolled by the COs, prisoners could come in and out of their dorms, or walk to the yard, or even go into another dormitory without supervision. There was less control over inmates' movements in Robeson Correctional than in the other prisons where Marell had been assigned.

Marell was overjoyed with the newfound freedom that comes when an inmate is held at the lowest custody level. He had "worked his way down" to the best situation an inmate can have in prison. He was no longer labeled a violent offender or a risk to public safety. And he got to wear the green uniform, a sign of minimum custody status that had been a long time coming.

If you have not been the mother of a convicted felon, you will have a hard time understanding how much this meant to me. I never feared that Marell could bring harm to us. But for more than twelve years, society and the prison system had classified him as dangerous. Now society officially viewed him as I did: not a threat. This was a big step forward for him, for me, and for our whole family. Our pride in Marell and in his advancement toward the end of his sentence pushed all of his other prison experiences out of mind. No matter how far the distance he had traveled away from us, no matter what he may have done, I always knew he was going to bring it on back. He had always said to me, "I remember my foundation, Ma." We were finally on the downhill slope.

And there was something else, something wonderful for all of us about Marell now being in minimum custody. We could bring him food each visit and sit down for a meal together. My health wasn't yet at full capacity, but nothing was going to keep me from Sunday dinner with my son for the first time in more than twelve years. So I asked him what he wanted me to prepare, and it did not take him long to decide. I should have known because he had often told me he imagined he could just taste my fried pork chops, mac and cheese, and steamed cabbage.

Visitation started right after church on Sunday, and like always, the first visit at a new facility made me extra nervous, so James, Sidnee, and I got there early. Marell had called a day before to explain the guidelines for bringing in food. Each item had to be in plastic containers or bags. I scoped out how the others had packed their food when we joined the line of visitors and was relieved that their packages all seemed similar to mine. There were big bags, small bags, and several Kentucky Fried Chicken containers. Inmates wouldn't care how they got their food or where it came from. They would be excited about eating anything that wasn't cooked in the prison.

After checking in, we could see Marell come out and secure a table for us while we waited for the COs to go through my containers. Yes, they went through each item with a fine-tooth comb. I had no problem with that, even when the food became a bit smashed, though not like it had been when it was inspected at Polk.

Marell eagerly watched as we proceeded to the table he had chosen. We came to realize that finding a table would be difficult if we did not arrive on time. And at times, we did have to share a table with other inmates and their families. Marell often became agitated when we had to sit with them. He was very selective, staying away from inmates he had problems with. And he didn't like it when some inmates' families would come from table to table, greeting each other. Once or twice, inmates—guys who recognized me from the rec center in Fayetteville—said hello. But that's as far as it went, socializing with other prisoners or their families. Luckily, on the day of our first meal with Marell, we had our own table, except for the yellowjackets flying around us. I normally hate eating outside because of the bugs, but that day, I didn't fuss at all. I wouldn't let anything ruin our celebration.

When we reached Marell, James was the first to hug him, and then Sidnee, and at last I did. "Are we going to eat, or what?" James remarked. So we all joined hands, as we always do at home, while James led us in prayer. Teary eyed, he thanked God for the blessing He was giving us, the blessing of being about to break bread with our son. "Recognize and count your blessings," James told him, "because this might not have happened. Think about the things we take for granted." When James finished, Marell laughed and said, "Let's eat, Pops!" Not even thinking about what I was doing, I began to fix plates just as I do at home. I'd brought decorative paper napkins and plates, and I filled Marell's plate as full as I could get it. I then fixed a plate for each of us.

Oh, what a joy to watch Marell eat! He chewed that food like it was the best that he'd ever had. James and Sidnee had no trouble eating either. But I just wanted to observe the whole thing. I looked forward to Marell's excitement after learning that I had baked his favorite, German chocolate cake. Now that was a meal like old times, a Sunday dinner as close as possible to the way it would be if we were all around our table at home.

It became my routine on Saturday afternoon to get a head start on my cooking. With lots of love, I would prepare the food, Marell's favorites and plenty of fruit like grapes, watermelon, and pineapple. He loved to have his snacks and these were healthy ones. That is until one Sunday, the COs irritated me by taking away the grapes. When I inquired why, one of them stated that some inmates were sneaking fruit to the dorms and fermenting it to make wine. What I had learned during Marell's years in prison was that sometimes the inmates assigned to take pictures during visits had the opportunity to smuggle in all sorts of contraband like cigarettes, cell phones, and even fruit. I hated that Marell's little joys were ruined because of those that would not follow rules. Yet when Marell seemed okay with this, it made me wonder if he was a part of the behind-the-scenes winery. And about the cell phone, I didn't want to know, but I'm sure that if he had one in Hoke he had one in Robeson.

Each week Marell received visits from friends and family members. Because he was so close to home, Kesia and Sidnee became more active visiting their brother, opening up a little breathing time for me. When they visited, I'd send them with funds to pick up a meal for Marell at a steakhouse or Chinese restaurant. Then there were my relatives who traveled from Texas to see Marell. When my sister Andrea and her son came up, they had a special weekday visit, and I drove down with them. I wasn't allowed in, so I parked where I could see them visiting and waved and blew kisses.

Just weeks after Marell made minimum, my dad visited. I always admired how he had supported Marell during these years in prison. Now, he could sit down and share a meal with his grandson. Marell told his Pa Pa about all of the diplomas and certificates that he had earned (in automotive systems, food service, masonry, and carpentry) and that he'd soon be assigned to a job at a vegetable market a few miles from the prison. A van would drop him off in the morning and pick him up in the afternoons; he was excited to do something besides hang out in the prison yard.

I always yearned for my parents to be proud of me and the children I had raised, so during Daddy's time with us, I had some bragging conversations with him about Kesia. She had worked so hard to pay off her law school debts and pass the bar exam. But she's a bull, and James and I always believed in her.

Kesia had formed a relationship with Marell before he went to prison, but Sidnee had gotten to know Marell by looking through a glass and seeing him in a prison uniform. Sidnee's whole growing up had been spent going with me to visit Marell. It was a natural thing for her. Even though he talked to her on the phone at least one time a week, there's a lot about a person you're not learning in that situation, and that worked both ways. Still, by the time she was a teenager, she knew enough to get stern with him when he did something she didn't approve of.

And now Sidnee was a rising senior in high school. Despite what she might say to him and how much they had been apart, Marell loved and admired his little sister. When he heard about a mentor program within the prison, Marell thought that this might be his way to attend Sidnee's graduation.

First, he would have to be approved for a program. The mentor, who could not be a relative, would also have to be approved by prison officials. That person would also have to take training classes at the prison on specific nights over a period of several weeks. Then the mentor could take the inmate off prison grounds to public places like a church or restaurant. Activities would be strictly timed for his arrival and return.

It was left up to the inmate to find the person willing to become a mentor, so Marell immediately began pulling names and contacting certain friends to volunteer for that role. I thought that perhaps a brother in our church would be a good choice, someone strong who could say "no" and mean it. But Marell had a friend who said *she* had a friend whose boyfriend would be a good mentor. Turns out, Marell and this boyfriend had gone all through elementary and high school together.

Marell contacted him, and the man led him to believe that he'd call Marell's prison caseworker and sign up for the program right away. Weeks went by, and the caseworker never got that call. Then more weeks passed when Marell couldn't track that man down. We were left hanging. As a result, Marell did not get a mentor while he was in Robeson Correctional, and he didn't go to Sidnee's graduation. I'm glad this was not a knockout blow to him. Yes, he was mad, but really more hurt than angry at his old friend's lack of loyalty and support.

For my part, I had never entertained the possibility that Marell could go to Sidnee's graduation. I don't know if the prison caseworker gave Marell any inkling of hope about going. But when I called to inquire—something I did just to satisfy Marell—I was told distinctly that he would never have been approved to attend an activity with family and friends.

More and more, Marell came up with ideas that I could see were not going to work out. He wanted to believe that since the graduation ceremony was a public event in a public place, he would have been allowed to go with a mentor. And I believed that things worked out for the right reason.

On June 10, 2009, James, Kesia, and other family members marveled with me when Sidnee walked across that stage. I teared up, realizing that Marell had missed his little sister grow from a baby girl to become a young lady. Here was our last child, getting ready to leave for college.

Kesia had graduated from high school a year after Marell got into trouble. When I was new at wrestling with how to deal with a son behind bars, I missed the time I could have had with her, helping her to apply to college and get scholarships. So with Sidnee, I was determined to get involved with all of the process. I did not want to let her down, the way I felt I had disappointed Kesia, though she never accused me of that.

When James and I suggested the University of North Carolina at Chapel Hill, where Kesia had gone to college, Sidnee immediately asserted her individuality. She was interested in North Carolina Central University in Durham and East Carolina University in Greenville, and she moved forward with these applications. She was doing everything on her own, even though we kept up regular conversations with her. But the University of North Carolina at Greensboro had not even been on her list of colleges, as far as we knew, and when she announced her decision to go there, we were all proud, especially Marell. He gave her pep talks, as if he knew the ropes of college life. He even bragged about his little sister to certain inmates sitting near us at the visits.

Acknowledging how proud he was of both sisters sometimes led him to admit aloud that he knew he had let me down. Yes, his path had disappointed his dad and me, and I had told him that, yet we were proud of what he had accomplished over the years. More important, we assured him that he could still be a good example to others who had done something wrong but turned their lives around.

EIGHTEEN

Too Much Freedom?

Marell called collect on July 14, 2009, to inform us that he had been moved again. This came as no surprise because several months earlier, he'd talked about signing up to be relocated to New Hanover Correctional Center in Wilmington, North Carolina.

One of the privileges that came with minimum security was that Marell could discuss with his caseworker going to prisons where he would have more freedom and opportunities for better jobs with higher pay. He wanted to earn money and save up for when he was released, and he seemed eager for a new level in his prison experience. But I wondered if he was ready for more freedom.

At first, I wasn't happy about extra time driving to get to see him, but the trip was a familiar one. Every summer I took kids from my rec center on outings to Fort Fisher and other places near Wilmington. On my first visit to New Hanover Correctional, when I got closer to the city and crossed the bridge, I had the sense that I was going to the beach. That would have been lovely because Kesia and Sidnee were in the car with me. Chatting and having all three of us together felt good. Visits to Marell with both my daughters were few and far between because they usually went to see him separately, catching a time when I was busy. I was a proud momma that day.

We stopped in Wilmington to get Marell the Chinese food he had asked for instead of a home-cooked meal. As usual, it was checked as we entered the gate. New Hanover Correctional had been a prison for nearly a hundred years; buildings had been updated or replaced, and new buildings were added in order to house nearly four hundred inmates while Marell was there. The place seemed like a typical prison.

But after walking in, I realized I had entered a large garden with tables and chairs. Big sunflowers leaned over the fence that separated the seating area from a field with tomato and banana plants and tall corn. Everything seemed green with life. I was amazed.

While the garden captured my attention, the girls went ahead to find a table, one of those picnic tables with attached seats that you had to step over in order to sit down. An umbrella (that was working, if we were lucky) kept the sun away. I waited to step into my seat because I wanted to be standing for a good steady hug with Marell, and he took his time coming out. Before he reached the table, we could smell his cologne from several feet away. He seemed overwhelmed to see both his sisters and grinned from ear to ear as he hugged them. They joked that he smelled like the whole bottle of cologne. Marell laughed and spent most of this visit talking to them. To see them eating all the food and enjoying one another, to have my children together—I'll never forget how they laughed that day. It would be a few years before we had another meal like that together.

Marell appeared to be adjusting to his new location, but he was getting fidgety and tired of lifting weights or playing basketball in the yard. "Some mess is always stirring," he said. He had been put on the list for a job, but many of the inmates were ahead of him, and his caseworker explained that it might be weeks before he got an assignment. I suggested that Marell take some courses, but he argued that he would only have to quit once a job came up. That did make sense, yet I worried about him having so much idle time.

On one of our first visits, Marell was about twenty minutes late coming out. I thought he was probably making himself look sharp for his dad and me. James had actually gotten up to inquire when he saw Marell coming across the yard. When he reached our table, he was furious. He said he never heard his name being called. Another inmate told him that he thought he had heard it. Marell said the COs were deliberately trying to mess with him, and he yelled to the CO in the visiting area that he was tired of this treatment. I pushed for Marell to let it go, and he eventually calmed down after James talked with him. Our visit turned out okay, but I got the feeling that this situation went further than the COs' not calling him loud enough.

After only three weeks, Marell was approved for work at a chicken processing plant about forty miles from New Hanover Correctional. I loved that he was going to be busy and constructive. Even though I couldn't shake the worry that this job would give him too much freedom, I thought my prayers had been answered. I purchased Dickies for his work clothes and shipped them to the prison. I also bought him some steel-toe boots that were checked through security when I came to a prison visitation. Once Marell started working, he needed a coat to keep warm because the plant was kept very cold for sanitary reasons. That coat was pretty expensive, so I called Daddy, and he immediately wired me the money for it. For the first time in more than thirteen years, Marell would be going out in public in something other than his prison uniform.

The job wasn't easy. He was on his feet all day cutting up chickens that came down an assembly line and were constantly being sprayed with water in order to wash away the blood and guts. That made the floor slick and especially dangerous for someone with a sharp knife in his hand, according to Marell the sharpest knife he'd ever held. When we'd visit him, we could see the cuts on his hands and arms that he'd gotten at work.

And as I had feared, the freedom he found at work created another kind of danger. Early one morning in May, there was a surprise shakedown in the prison. Before that, Marell had been lucky because I only remember one other shakedown in a different correctional center where he had been busted with too many snack items. Then the COs knew he had been hustling, using these items like cash to gamble during card games. So they drained Marell dry of all the snacks he had in his cell.

But this time at New Hanover, a phone was found near his bed. Marell denied that it was his. Because he lived in a dormitory situation, he claimed there were people in and out of that area all the time, that it could be anybody's phone. In my Mother's Day card, he wrote, "Ma, I didn't mean to let you down or disappoint you. It seems like the harder I try to do the right thing, the more I keep coming up on the short end of the stick whether it's my fault or not." He sounded convincing, so I was willing to give him the benefit of a doubt, but I knew for a fact he had had a cell phone in Hoke Correctional. And I also knew for certain that work release created all sorts of opportunities for prisoners to obtain contraband.

Even though the phone could not be traced, Marell's excuses did not fly with the administration, and he was charged with illegal contraband. He was still allowed to go to work at the plant, but he couldn't have visits, canteen use, or phone calls for thirty days. This gave him time to think and pay attention to what I wrote: "Son, you have come too close to have your whole plan go backwards." "Ma," he wrote back, "thank you for always believing in me. I do not know what I would do without your support." He promised "to work real hard to stay out of trouble." Prison was not the place where he wanted to spend the rest of his life.

Still, despite his promises, I worried that Marell had made the COs mad by stirring things up. Every now and then, he'd tell us that they had their inmate favorites and had something against him for thinking he was so smart and popular. Marell boasted that he got along with mostly everyone, especially with the female COs. And as the weeks passed, I noticed he appeared so sure of himself, so happy-go-lucky. This was not the cockiness he'd shown in Lanesboro where it was all about his sense of power and control among the inmates. At New Hanover, his confidence came from having the attention of women.

Marell bragged about his relationships with female workers at the plant. How was he able to spend so much time with these ladies? Well, the van dropped him off maybe thirty minutes before clock-in. Security was not very tight, as long as he was in place for check-in and check-out. Marell learned how to work the system from other inmates who had gotten good at it. So all in all, he liked his job, and the rewards that came with it—the ladies who were bringing him meals and other items against prison policy, I am sure. He thought he was just the man!

His contract at the plant was supposed to last several months. If he worked hard and followed rules, he might get another contract period. But Marell got complaints from his supervisors every week, and he felt they were a little salty because one of the females on the assembly line was paying him extra attention. Right after Marell discussed the situation with me, he was written up for an incident on the job, something about machine safety, and he was suspended for two weeks. That supervisor also reprimanded the female worker who had been talking with Marell.

"Ma, I didn't do nothing," he said at our next visit. Still, I advised him to forget explaining his side and just take the two-week suspension. I feared that making a big deal of it would possibly lead to an investigation of the other situation, the one with the woman. So Marell kept his mouth closed and sat out for those weeks.

But when he returned to the plant, the job never went smooth again. Even though Marell complained regularly, he gladly accepted the overtime hours to put more money in his account. He talked about stacking money so that when he walked out of prison he wouldn't have to face the world broke.

Marell was always so organized with his papers that even now I can see from his "Temporary Work Release Earning Receipts" and paycheck stubs that he worked between July 20, 2009, and February 21, 2010. He started at $7.75 an hour, just a little above the $7.25 minimum wage that year. By the end of September, he was making $8.25 an hour, and by the end of November $8.75. This was much better pay than the $1.00 or $2.00 a day he got for any of the jobs he'd had inside the prison.

But not everything Marell made went into that account. Federal tax was withheld, and the Department of Correction took out $10.00 for his transportation to work each way, every day; that was a total of $100.00 every week. Marell had to pay the DOC for his room and board while he was working. And he also figured out how he could use some of his money to help me with what I spent on collect calls from him.

Maybe it was my pride; I didn't like to think I could use that help. And I didn't want to go through the trouble of documenting all my calls. This was back when long distance calls cost more than local ones and phone bills showed who every call was to and how long it took.

But Marell fussed and fussed at me. "Ma, that's one way I can help you. It's my money. I earned it. I want to help you." So finally I sent the phone bill to the DOC office in Raleigh that regulated prison accounts. And Marell wrote to them that it was a struggle for us to pay for all his collect calls. Finally we did get two checks from the DOC, one for $180.00 and another for $200.00.

Marell was so proud of getting that money sent to me, to hear him talk, you'd think he was paying my mortgage. I wasn't unappreciative, but to me, it wasn't about the dollars and cents. It was about his feeling that he was finally helping us. That was a very big issue for him.

So what with one thing or another taken out of Marell's account, that stacking of money he had hoped for never happened. And at the end of his contract with the chicken processing plant, he was not asked to come back.

Once again, Marell was determined to make a fresh start. So he enrolled in a beginning telecommunications class at the nearby community college. Another inmate named Darian had already taken this course, and he befriended Marell by helping him study and steering him in a positive direction.

Darian was also working outside the prison at an electrical company. He realized that Marell's training might qualify him for a job in the same place and helped him to get hired. Whenever we spoke to Marell on the phone or at a visitation, he talked about how much he enjoyed his job experience. He loved this electrical work and the fact that *he* understood it, but *we* did not. His contract was only for four months, but he hoped that a second one would be offered. Unfortunately, when the contract period ended, there was not enough work at the company for Marell to stay on.

This came as a blow to him, particularly since Darian was now preparing for his release date and had negotiated a permanent position at that electrical company. Marell did not hold this against him because there hadn't been any backstabbing. Darian was just a nice guy who simply knew how to do the job better and would be available soon for full time work.

And now again, Marell was eager for a fresh start. How many times I've said that! Looking back, I realize that as many times as he faced setbacks, he always held on. I may be late giving him credit, but I say now that it takes a mighty strong person to keep hoping for positive things in his life when there are so many setbacks.

And that's how Darian came into the picture again. Marell trusted him enough to ask him to become his mentor. "Wait a minute," I said when Marell told me about his plan, "there's something strange about that. Darian is an inmate!" Yes, but the prison administration had approved him. Matter of fact, Marell's caseworker spoke so highly of Darian that she said he had been a model prisoner.

So while Darian was still in prison, he began the process of becoming a mentor by agreeing to take the required training once he was released. This would involve evening classes that lasted about an hour or an hour-and-a-half for around six weeks. We were impressed that Darian would do that. You'd think that once he got out of prison, he'd want to stay as far away from it as possible.

Once Darian completed the training, James and I arranged to meet him in a parking lot of a Food Lion around the corner from the prison the next time we were in Wilmington for a visit with Marell. Darian told me what kind of car he'd be driving, and we spotted it immediately. He told us he was happy to have his freedom because his wife and children needed him. His child was in the car too. Darian seemed sincere when he talked about taking care of his family, and I thought it was so admirable of him to take on the extra responsibility of mentoring Marell.

And I felt relieved when Darian said, "Marell's got game." That showed me Darian knew he'd have to be strong. "Do not let Marell persuade or connive you in any way," I warned, and I thanked Darian over and over. I promised to send him money so that he'd have whatever he needed to spend on mentoring Marell. Before we said goodbye, we exchanged phone numbers. My son was a grown man, yet I still wanted to be able to call Darian randomly to inquire how everything was going.

Church was the good place to be, and that was where Marell went on his first trip outside the prison with Darian. I had mailed my son a pair of slacks and shirt so he would appear presentable. I imagined how handsome he would look; I could almost see and feel the grin on his face. I was somethin' happy.

It gave me energy and comfort to know that he was going to church and that he was not in a uniform. For the first time since February 4, 1996, he would be out in public and not labeled in any way as a prisoner—no uniform, no guards, no handcuffs, no shackles, no inmate van dropping him off like it did at work release. This was a big step in the direction of his re-entry into the world.

On the way to New Covenant Church in downtown Wilmington, Darian called me from his car. His family was with him, and he allowed Marell to speak to me. We didn't talk long, but Marell assured me that when they were headed back, they would call again. And they did. In a few weeks, Darian was even given permission to take Marell to dinner after church.

This routine of Sunday phone calls, and Darian taking Marell to church and out to eat, went on for a couple of months. Then, on Sunday morning September 10th, Darian called while I was in church. When I saw his number on my cell, I stepped outside to answer. Something must be wrong.

"Mrs. Williams, it's all my fault. I tried to tell them, but they did not listen. They took him back to the place." All I could hear was Darian's frantic voice, apologizing over and over.

"I don't blame you, but tell me, what happened? Where is Marell? Who took him?" I tried to calm Darian down because I wanted him to get to the point. Who had taken Marell? Where? Was this like when the police charged Marell with possession of drugs and took him from Harnett County Correctional to the jail? Darian was so upset he could not give a clear answer.

I immediately called New Hanover Correctional and was told I would have to wait until Monday to speak with Marell's caseworker. At least I was relieved to know that he was still at that prison and that he hadn't been taken anywhere else.

But before I could talk to the caseworker on Monday, Darian called me again. He was clearer now and explained what had happened. With Marell in his car, he had made a detour to a McDonald's drive-through. This made them twenty minutes late for their scheduled 11:00 arrival at church. A lieutenant from the sheriff's department was already there to conduct a routine inmate check. When Darian pulled into the parking lot, the officer immediately handcuffed Marell and took him back to prison. Anyone in the parking lot who had also been late for service now saw Marell not as another churchgoer but as someone in cuffs, a prisoner.

Darian said he would write a letter, make a statement, do anything to clear this up, and when I got Marell's caseworker on the phone that morning, she confirmed that Darian had been calling and was willing to take all the blame. But I didn't get any comfort from talking to her. Matter of fact, when I got off the phone I felt sick because she thought Marell would be charged with trying to escape. This A6 charge is one of the worst a prisoner can receive, and he was immediately sent to the hole while we waited for an investigation to take place and the evidence presented to a hearing board. I hated that the system was treating my son as an escapee.

Over the years that Marell had been away, I had sometimes put my worries in the trouble box. In my mind, that was a place for things I decided not to deal with. Then there were times I put my troubles in the Lord's hands and said, "You're in control." At other times, I took action as a way to feel that I was in control. I didn't have an outline of how I handled situations, a plan in advance about what went into the trouble box, what I gave to the Lord, and what I handled myself. But now I knew this situation with Marell had to be reviewed and understood the way I saw it, the way Darian and Marell said it had happened that Sunday morning. So I took action, something I had not done for a while, and started writing to the Department of Correction.

Marell also began writing letters to the warden and to the DOC. I never saw those letters, but I guess they were like the one he wrote to me about that side trip to McDonald's: "It was his decision solely. . . . if he chooses to deviate from the schedule, I'm in a lose-lose situation. He took responsibility for his mistake, yet I'm in the hole. I'm not going to lay down for something I didn't do no matter the consequences . . . . Hopefully logic and justice will prevail."

Marell drilled down on his innocence and refused to plead guilty, and I did not give up writing letters and making calls. But nothing happened for weeks. And then, everything was dropped. Come to find out, Marell had never been charged with an A6, trying to escape. The officer who had taken Marell into custody at the church had recommended only a B12 for failing "to adhere to approved schedules for community-based programs." But Marell was never even officially charged with that, probably because Darian stood up for him, and because Marell and I wrote letters and made calls. But for weeks, I'd feared that Marell might be found guilty of trying to escape and have his sentence extended for years. I had feared the worst, all because that caseworker was misinformed or was careless about telling me the facts. Why couldn't she just have said we needed to wait and see? Why did she talk about something when she didn't know what she was talking about?

Marell had been scared too, but his fear came out as anger and an attitude. This is what I thought might happen when Uncle Felton died, that Marell would take his sorrow out on other prisoners or guards. An inmate can't be scared or sad, but he can be mad.

And Marell was mad. During the waiting period, he'd been in the hole, he had missed visitations, and he had lost privileges. He even had the nerve to suggest that he should be allowed to continue the mentor program. "Son," I said, "you've got to pick and choose your battles. Don't make any waves."

This was just one more time that I reminded him of God's mercy and grace. I showed my thankfulness by shouting to Marell, to myself, to anyone I talked to about it, to anyone who would listen: "God is so good to us!" I praised God and continued to praise him, and when I prayed, I asked for strength to deal with what came my way.

By now the weather had gotten colder and visitation was held in the cafeteria. The tables and benches were the very long rectangular ones, like the kind I remember were used in Sidnee's grade school. Unless you were the person lucky to be on the very end, you had to do some hopping to get seated on the bench. I was having trouble with my back due to an accident when I fell at work, so I'd have to put my right leg over the bench, steady myself, and then swing my left in.

This seating arrangement was always snug, shoulder-to-shoulder with the next person, whether that person was in our family or a stranger. Their loud talking prevented us from hearing one another at times. This situation irritated Marell. He did not like it at all, and he said he was so tired of this place. I whispered to him that anyone who had female COs bringing him his choice of food every week was doing okay.

He responded quickly, "Ma, even that gets old."

NINETEEN
Risky Relationships

I understood that just because the COs didn't find the proof of some charge, that didn't mean Marell wasn't guilty of something. There was a difference between provable and feasible.

It was feasible to me that Marell would have a cell phone at New Hanover because I knew that he had one at Hoke. Still, I had given him the benefit of the doubt when he was charged with that contraband. When he was suspended from the plant for a safety violation, I didn't think he was at fault, at least not for that. I absolutely knew he was not guilty of trying to escape, even when the caseworker said he might be charged with an A6. And before Marell left New Hanover Correctional, he was taken into administrative custody again for another violation. We were in another fight for his innocence. At least this was Marell's take on the situation.

Smoking had been banned in all of North Carolina's seventy-six prisons since late in 2005. Withdrawing from cigarettes made for some mighty edgy and angry inmates, and those who wanted to smoke found ways to do it. One morning, the COs confiscated a lighter and cigarettes in the shower area while Marell was there, and he was charged with a B16, the possession of tobacco products, paraphernalia, unauthorized lighters, or lighting devices. Like he had before, he claimed that many inmates came in and out and the contraband could have been left by anyone. He had spent several weeks in the hole during an investigation of this incident before another inmate admitted that the cigarettes and lighter were his and that he had put them under a mat before Marell came into the shower.

I couldn't get a grasp on what was actually true. I wanted to believe that Marell was doing everything right. And I wanted believe that the COs were doing everything right. But I knew that guards sometimes set people up. Marell used to say that guards could do anything to those inmates who don't have a family to look out for them. Could Marell have been set up with that B16 charge, even though he was cleared of it?

"Ma, we are on our last leg," he would tell me. But sadly, I questioned his statement because in the twenty months that he had spent in New Hanover Correctional, he'd been involved in too many incidents that he'd wiggled out of. I feared his road could take a wrong turn so close to the end of his sentence. I knew he was pushing his luck.

Marell also had other situations going on, risky relationships that he'd managed to hide from the authorities. He'd done other things that could have gotten him charged with trying to escape, that could have sent him back to medium, and that would have added years on to his sentence. Like what was going on with that CO at New Hanover who was getting him whatever he wanted in the way of a meal. My son had been in prison nearly fourteen years, and I was aware that New Hanover Correctional was not the first prison where female COs had bought him meals or shown all sorts of interest in him. When it came to Marell, race was never an issue.

At times the attentions of these women had gone way beyond treating Marell to special food. At one correctional center, he had been approached by several women COs who found opportunities to speak privately with him. In one case, this talking led to a particular woman bringing Marell contraband items of food and money, and giving me a gift card to Walmart and trinkets for Sidnee. This particular woman was somewhat older than my son and so heavy her stomach hung out over the belt of her uniform. But she was a totally pleasant person. How do I know? Because Marell gave her my phone number. She'd call to check on me and ask if I needed anything.

During one call, she said to me, "Ms. Williams, I told him that I love him," but she was afraid he had someone else. "He's my son," I said to her, "but I have to tell you, there's nothing he can give you. He's got to take care of himself." Still, she was determined to make Marell happy. But he saw an opportunity here, not a romance. He recognized her weakness and used her low self-esteem to his advantage. He had the gift of saying just what a person wanted to hear, saying things that made her feel good and important. And she was happy that a guy was paying attention to her. I think she really fell in love with Marell because even after she stopped working with the Department of Correction, she kept in touch with him.

At another prison, it was Marell who became interested in a female CO. He didn't care about getting privileges or items from her and talked about how special she was. Marell was really falling for her. When I warned him that this relationship could lead to danger, he responded that he would be careful.

Soon they began to exchange letters. Marell had no expectation of privacy in any letter he wrote, except to his attorney, so all other letters were considered non-privileged mail that could be opened for inspection. To keep their secret, Marell called her by a made-up name in letters he addressed to her at our home. Using that name, she wrote back. For a while, his letters arrived nearly every day, and I met her personally when she came to my house weekly to pick them up. There were times when he would call when she was there just so that they could speak to each other. I had nothing to do with arranging these calls. All I knew in advance was that she'd be at my house at a certain time.

How the mind plays tricks! The soul mellows. What's abnormal or wrong begins to seem normal or right. In a crazy way, it did seem like a normal kind of worry, to worry about my son and his relationship with a woman. If she was keeping him occupied, then he wasn't getting into worse trouble. He wasn't being cut up by violent inmates. He wasn't being thrown into the hole. So I got tangled up, and I didn't know when to get out. I soothed my conscience by telling myself that I was not helping him do something really bad, like selling drugs. And I actually allowed this situation to go on under my nose because I wanted to please my son. It was making him happy.

Because we knew phone conversations were not privileged, and at any point the guards can listen in, I never used her real name when I talked to Marell on the phone or in letters when I wrote to him. But at visits, I constantly spoke my opinion.

"Are you crazy? This relationship could lengthen your prison time. She could lose her job. What about her children?" And I was afraid that I could have been charged with something. When I told Marell the whole thing made me nervous, he just blew me off: "Ma, you always have to be so squeaky clean."

One evening, I spoke to this woman when she came by to pick up Marell's letters. "He is my son," I told her, "but he's not worth losing your livelihood. He has nothing to offer you—no money, no future." But she stood her ground and explained that her feelings for Marell were serious.

This went on for months until finally Marell heard talk amongst the inmates that there might be something going on between them. And some of the COs were asking her about Marell. She denied a relationship with him, but he was becoming uneasy about the gossip. So that whole thing wound down before it blew up.

And while Marell was working at the chicken processing plant, he took risks with a co-worker that could have gotten him an A6 for real. Any time he was anywhere except for his assigned post, he could have been charged with trying to escape. When Marell had been charged with that safety violation and the woman had been reprimanded for talking too much with him, well, the supervisor may or may not have known that the situation had actually gone beyond flirting. That's why I had told Marell not to fight his two-week suspension.

Marell didn't need any more light shining on him, or her. Their relationship was getting out of control. She became so fixed on Marell that even after he was transferred out of New Hanover Correctional, she traveled to visit him at a different prison.

There was also another woman who worked at the plant. She went so far as to tell Marell that she and her husband hadn't been getting along for a while, and that she'd leave the man for my son.

Marell told me about these women and a few others. And I have since learned that there were many, many more that I did not know about, women who were so attracted to him that they threw themselves at him even though he was behind bars.

Because Marell kept all the letters he received in prison and organized them neatly in boxes, I have now seen hundreds of letters that came from at least twenty-one different women. Many letters were full of things that were distasteful and even could be considered X-rated. I had a hard time believing that young ladies would think, let alone put on paper, this trash.

Then there were caring, heartfelt letters, like the ones that came from a girl he met just once in high school when he had visited my mother in Texas. Others came from a neighborhood girl that I saw all the time even though I had no idea she was writing to my son. Another girl wrote that she told her boyfriend he had to understand her special relationship with Marell. And another asked his permission to do things and to get certain clothes, hairdos, piercings, and tattoos.

I counted more than sixty-five envelopes with the words "I love you" written on them. Many envelopes were well decorated with lipstick kisses. Several girls used Marell's last name as their last name on their return addresses, as if they were married to him. They called themselves his wife and promised to be devoted until the end. They dreamed that they would be together. They fantasized about when Marell would get out. But they had no grasp on reality, and no knowledge that there was more than one woman dreaming this same dream. He was their world, but only in imagination. How could he be their world if they never saw him?

Poor girls! Where were their mothers, guardians, grandmothers, or somebody to steer them better? I could not, would not read every letter. My brain would have burst. I had heard stories about situations like this, but I never guessed they would become so personal.

And I never, ever knew that Marell was having these relations with so many women through their letters. But if this crazy stuff made him happy and comforted him, I am okay with it. The letters were really harmless.

TWENTY
Home Visits

2011 had come in pretty rough for me. I was having bi-weekly appointments with a pain management doctor. Back pain was affecting my movement and ability to take care of normal chores. Driving long distances and sitting for two hours in the car made the pain worse. Sometimes, after traveling to visit Marell, I had to spend the next day in bed.

So when on April 12, 2011, I received a call from him that he had been moved back to Robeson County Correctional, the words sounded sweet to my soul and to my back.

Marell seemed happy and immediately talked about his eligibility for home visits. "Hold your horses, son," I said. "How did you get moved back to Robeson after having all that trouble in New Hanover? Are you going to be on any restrictions here?" Marell reminded me that they'd never found any sound proof of his involvement in wrongdoing. Matter of fact, he had already entered into a discussion with his caseworker about getting home visits. Marell spoke like they would begin the next week. But it took months from beginning the approval process to the day of his first visit home.

Family, work, and now Marell coming home for visits. Was I ready for this next stage? During the next few weeks, I suffered from a nervous stomach and anxiety.

We'd had an empty nest for years, except for PJ, our little dachshund that we had adopted recently from Sidnee. She came home only every other weekend, and Kesia had her own place. Now Marell would be having two day passes and one overnight visit each month until the time he was released. There was a big difference between seeing to his welfare in prison—visiting him, writing letters and making calls when he needed something, thinking and praying about him every day—and taking responsibility for him at home. More than the empty nest was being affected. This mother was pure scared.

I realized that the person who would be coming home was someone I didn't know. He had been away for over fifteen years. He was no longer the boy that I had raised. He had grown into a man under prison regulations, and he had adjusted to the behavior of other inmates. "Ma, this is a different world in here," he always said. His habits were no longer formed to our ways.

I knew that I would have the responsibility of standing watch on Marell every minute during two separate eight-hour visits and one twenty-four-hour overnight visit per month. That meant three weekends a month would be out of our normal schedule. If I would need to do an errand, James would have to cut into his weekend work on lawns. During an overnight visit, I'd have to work out with James to be at home on Sunday morning if I wanted go to church. Would I even be able to take a nap during the day? It would be like having a child in the house that couldn't be left alone or unsupervised.

I felt ashamed to be thinking this way about a son, my son whom I loved with all my heart. I kept my feelings hidden from everyone but my husband. "Marell will be fine" was all James said. He didn't understand my worry, but I felt that I saw things he could not, and after discussing them with him, I did more soul-searching. I prayed hard for strength to be able to deal with this new relationship with Marell. Would I have to get into sergeant mode, enforcing rules? Would I still be the mother that Marell loved, who was doing everything right?

During our regular Sunday visits to the prison, home visits were a conversation piece for Marell. James and I learned we would have to fill out an application that would first go through the prison caseworker at Robeson County Correctional. He was a very nice man, though I can't remember his name. Then the application would go through Ms. Shirley Peterkin. She took care of paperwork for home visits at several minimum security prisons in Robeson County. Finally, the RCC caseworker and a DOC staff member would inspect our home.

A couple of months went by. Then Marell handed me an application form during one of our Sunday visits. James and I had to supply our home address and social security numbers as well as information about where we worked. We also answered questions about how we would handle certain situations, like what we would do if the inmate left the premises. We would immediately call the prison, we answered, and we also let Marell know that's what would happen if he ever tried to leave our home.

Marell told me that his caseworker and a DOC staff person would inspect our home as soon as I filed our application. This I did. But about two weeks passed before his caseworker contacted me with one or two questions. We also went over my answer about what I'd do if Marell left home. Finally, the caseworker set a date for inspection the following week.

The day before the inspectors came, I dusted the furniture, vacuumed, and mopped floors. I even tasked James to cut the grass. I wanted everything to go right. James said I was making too much over this visit. "It's only so much they will be checking for," he said, so nonchalant. But before leaving for work on the morning of the inspection, we did an inventory to check all areas of our home.

Our appointment had been scheduled at noon, around our lunch hour so that we wouldn't have to take time off from work. James and I returned to the house about thirty minutes early. To our surprise, the caseworker and Mr. Luther Chavis, a DOC staffer in plain clothes, pulled into the driveway right behind us. We walked into the house together and sat down in the living room. I offered them a glass of water, one of them accepted, and we began to talk.

Mr. Chavis immediately commented to James about him being a fisherman. From that, I gathered they had viewed James's fishing poles in the back yard, and I shot him a look. So, they had been to the house before we arrived. I controlled my reaction to what felt like an invasion of our privacy and saved my comments for James after they left: "The nerve of them. They were pure in our backyard when we weren't home."

The men also told us that they had spoken to a few neighbors earlier. We did not question who those neighbors had been, but apparently they were okay with Marell coming to our residence and had no fear of him. They also mentioned that James and I were good parents and nice neighbors. We were happily surprised that they went out of their way to say good things about us.

But that wasn't how neighbors always reacted, Mr. Chavis told us. Some people said they would be afraid of an inmate. And there were other reasons why the inspectors might deny a family home visits. Mr. Chavis said in one house there was so much hoarding that the inspectors couldn't even get in.

Actually, we had a comfortable, social conversation with these men. They laughed and talked with us for about twenty minutes, complimenting us on Marell's upbringing. The caseworker shared several conversations that he'd had with Marell, and Mr. Chavis made us feel good when he acknowledged that no matter how hard you try, your children do not always follow the path that was set for them.

All that preparation, and the gentlemen never went past the living room!

The easy part was over. We had been approved; now we had to wait on Marell to get approval. I could not sit around twiddling my fingers, and I advised him, "Don't sneeze unless you really have to." He could not let anything ruin the approval process.

Still waiting, after a couple of weeks, I began to call the caseworker, and then I spoke to Ms. Peterkin. She assured me that it would not be long. I felt that she was really concerned and trusted that soon Marell could start his home visits. By the third week in July, she called me at work to say that Marell would be able to visit the following weekend.

I screamed with joy, and after covering my summer camp responsibilities with the proper staff, I took early lunch break. Even though it was the beginning of the week, I was hyped to start preparing all the things that I wanted to cook for Marell. I headed to Walmart and put whatever I thought he would like in my grocery basket 'til it nearly burst over and felt heavy to push. As I approached the register, Marell's fourth grade teacher, who was now a county commissioner, joined the line behind me.

"How's my boy?" she asked. I had not seen her in years, but this is how she always asked about Marell from the time he was in school and throughout his prison years.

"He'll be coming home for a visit this weekend!" I responded. We held up the progress of the line with our hugs of joy, and even the cashier chimed in to congratulate me.

"Marell was always special to me," the commissioner said. "Please give me a call to let me know how everything goes. Here's my card." This was a connection, maybe even an opportunity for Marell when he got out, or so I thought at the moment. This was really happening. My son would be visiting home Saturday!

But my excitement was cut short. Once I returned to the rec center, a staff member informed me that I had received a call from Robeson County Correctional. The caller left no name, yet when I returned the call, I asked for Ms. Peterkin.

"Is this Mrs. Williams?" asked the officer who answered the phone. "Yes," I answered. Then he relayed the message from Ms. Peterkin. Marell's visit was not approved, and the officer was not sure why.

"No, no! I need to speak with somebody to explain why."

"We understand, ma'am."

"Do you?" I screamed. "Do you know what it is to have children? Can you imagine how I feel now?" Why hadn't my son been approved for home visits? I began to cry, and the rest of the afternoon was miserable. There I was with over $200.00 spent on food, money I could have used on bills. Ms. Peterkin was avoiding me. I felt drained.

Finally, next morning, she called. She started off by apologizing for not talking to me herself. She said that she could not bear to hear how emotional and terribly disappointed I would be, but the prison board had decided that Marell had not served enough time in minimum custody before the home visit could be approved.

"How much more time did he need?" I asked. I got no concrete answer, and the call ended.

This was the second time in less than a year that my emotions had been whipped around by poor communication from DOC staff members. At New Hanover, the caseworker had told me Marell would be charged with trying to escape when this was not the charge that had been recommended. And surely Ms. Peterkin or someone should have known how much time Marell needed at minimum before a home visit could be approved. Because these people weren't clear in communicating, or caring enough, or on top of their jobs, they added to my anxiety. They need to say what is correct, or just say, "I don't know." People suffer from wrong information.

Ms. Peterkin was still apologizing three weeks later when she called again, now to inform me that Marell had been approved. I did my apologizing too, for the way I had gone off on her, but I had to ask, "Are you for sure this time? I could not take that pain again." "Yes," she answered.

Marell's home visit for the very next weekend was on and popping. I told him to keep it low key, yet I bragged to all I talked to.

Marell will be here for a day! Yes, Marell is coming home, so get ready!

Saturday, September 17, 2011. Looking back, I remember that I had prepared for Marell more like he was a visitor than my son.

James, Sidnee, and I drove almost in silence the thirty minutes to Robeson Correctional. I am sure we were all wondering about the same things. What will we talk about with Marell? What will we do? How will he adjust to having family around him after all this time? Family and close friends. I knew Marell had sent the word out to his friends. How would we deal with them coming to our house? And how would Marell take coming home to us and then having to return to confinement? Was this going to be a positive experience for him or not? Was this going to be a positive experience for *us*?

Upon arriving at the prison, Sidnee waited on a bench outside while James and I entered on a different side than usual, the side with the warden's office. We informed the CO at the desk that we had come to check Marell Williams out. Then that officer handed us a yellow four-inch-wide slip marked with checkout and return times, and a space for signatures. We were the only people who could pick Marell up and bring him back.

"Handle this with your life," the CO told us, "Marell Williams cannot return without this slip." I took the CO seriously even though he did not say what would happen if Marell returned without it. We had learned our lesson in Wilmington.

We joined Sidnee back outside, and before long, we saw Marell walking across the yard. Other inmates were holding up their clenched fists in the power sign and yelling things like, "You got it, Boone!" "I got you!" "Have a good visit!" "We happy for you, Boone." But were they really, I wondered? Which one of these inmates meant him well? Which one was jealous and would be happy to see him mess up?

As Marell approached, we saw that he was wearing the pair of brown jeans and the checkered shirt I had bought him when we expected his home visit back in July. Now he was getting to wear these clothes at last. We could also see that he was chatting and laughing with the CO who was escorting him. That officer did seem really happy for Marell and wished him a nice visit.

The next minute, Sidnee and I each grabbed one of his arms and held on until we reached the car. James got his hug before going to the driver's door. Then Marell slid into the back seat with Sid, and before we were even good out of the parking lot, he joked, "Can I drive?" James laughed, "Boy, are you crazy!" Soon Marell asked to see my cell phone-something new to him because it took pictures. Sid had her cell too, and they spent most of the ride switching phones and taking selfies.

Because we had been warned to travel nowhere other than to and from our house, we had mapped out the longest route so that Marell could see what Fayetteville looked like after all his years away. We knew at any time we could be followed by an officer from the prison. Officers might randomly check the house to see if Marell was where he was supposed to be. They could also check to see if he was around any beer, wine, drugs, or weapons. All of that was fine because James and I were going to follow every rule.

I had made sure everything would be just right at the house, and when we pulled into the driveway, Marell said, "Pops, the yard looks good." And once we were out of the car, I just couldn't keep my hands off Marell. That didn't bother him because he was always affectionate and liked to be hugged, but James said, "Let the boy breathe." Soon Kesia joined us, which made it so much like old times.

But was it really? Really like old times?

We were afraid to overwhelm Marell, so we gave him space, and he went straight to his room. Of course, it had changed. There was not a single piece of furniture in it that had been there when he went away. But still hanging on the wall was what Marell had carved in his ninth-grade shop class, that piece of wood with the words "Boone's Place." "It's my room," he said, and he landed straight on the bed with my phone still in his hand.

When Marell came out, James had already left for his weekend job. So it was just Marell with the girls and me in conversation, catching him up on our family and changes around Fayetteville. We chatted about everything, yet about nothing heavy. He was coming into our world, *the* world. We were very selective about picking our topics.

There were several visitors that afternoon including two young ladies. One of them—I'll call her Gladys—had met Marell at a former workplace. For several months, she had been visiting him in prison where we had already met her. At times, we all visited Marell together, and she and her mother even came to Thanksgiving dinner at our home the year before.

Even still, Marell seemed low key, often appearing distant with her and the rest of his company. He cut time short with outside visitors because I insisted that they had to go. I wanted him to get settled and eat, and then leave on time for Robeson Correctional. Too soon James and I were preparing to take him back. We wanted nothing to go wrong with this first visit so he arrived at the prison a few minutes ahead of scheduled check-in. Eight hours at home and thirty minutes driving each way. That was nine straight hours that we had with Marell, the longest time we'd been with him since that February day in 1996.

I sat in the car while James walked Marell to the office. Returning home, I felt sad and empty. He had been shown tenderness and consideration at home. In prison, there was no one who cared about his needs, no one to offer him some grape Kool-Aid or fix his favorite foods. This is the kind of thing family members do for each other. But in prison, he'd be eating the same old slop that everybody else was eating.

I knew that Marell was a grown man, but he was still my child. To leave your child in prison and know that you are free? You would think that after fifteen years I would have gotten used to it. But it was harder to bring him back after he had been home than it was to say goodbye after visiting him at prison.

I wondered if my emotions upon leaving Marell were the same as he felt leaving us. He never said, and I never asked. Things had been normal during his visit home, then he returned to the abnormal. We knew, though we didn't talk about it, that when he passed through the prison doors he would have to face the body cavity search, then the noise and crowding of other inmates. He had described this in the past and told us how much he hated it. Wouldn't you?

In many ways, every one of Marell's visits home was like this first. As we approached our yard, I would enjoy seeing him smile. I would want the neighbors to see us: "Look how far we have come! Lord, I thank you." And I would try for both of the girls to be there with me and James. We were always proud to have Marell home.

Marell didn't want me to cook a lot of food or invite many people over during his visits because he knew I was having worse problems with my back. Though I agreed to invite only close family, friends from the neighborhood did get the word when Marell was coming. They would stop by, and he would step out on the porch to chat. Yes, that *was* like old times. And like always, I wanted to see everyone who graced my porch.

If Marell stood by his friend's ride at the street, I watched. "Miss Roz, you sure ain't changed," said one of them. True enough. Who knew what someone might hand Marell that he'd try to take back to prison? James would say to me, "You huffin' and puffin' isn't going to keep him from taking some contraband." But through a friend whose relative worked in a prison, I had heard that sometimes an inmate or a guard might want to trip a person up right before he's released. They'd want to get him in trouble so that he'd have more years tacked on to his sentence.

Marell was too close to being free for me to let up. I had worked hard for this moment; I was determined to protect my son. Even still, I had flipped the switch on my worrying. I had learned when to put it in the trouble box because I knew that getting out of prison had to be what *he* wanted more than what *I* wanted.

Each time Marell came home, I tried to make him comfortable. But I noticed that he did not eat everything, even though I had prepared the food he enjoyed. Sometimes he complained that his stomach was nervous, and the food did not go down smoothly. He ate in spurts. Finally he admitted that on a few occasions, what he ate, he had to throw up.

That made me sad and worried. What would I do if he got really sick while he was home? I decided that I would call the prison first, then I'd call 911. I wanted to have a plan for whatever might happen.

And I actually cried when I learned he threw up the favorites I had spent days preparing. To cook for my family, to have so much food, to have them enjoy it—this was a ritual that pleased me. Yet, I understood. This was Marell's home; at the same time, it was a new setting for him. He would have to learn how to relax in it because I saw how tense and uneasy he was, starting with his very first visit.

When we stood in the yard, he constantly watched everything. I would be talking, but Marell would be looking at any movement around him. When I asked him about this, he replied, "Ma, in that place, you have to watch everything. It's almost like you have to sleep with one eye closed and the other open."

During the weekend of his first overnight visit, he invited Gladys to our home. I had no problem with that, but a problem came up, when Marell asked if she could stay over. He gave the excuse that it had gotten too late for her to drive to her home an hour and a half away. "We are still the conservative, old fashioned parents that raised you," I said. Our answer was "No," and "No" was our final answer. And that was the last time I saw Gladys.

That night, after she left, Marell went to his room. With me being a light sleeper, I could hear him talking on the phone all night long. I do not know if it was with her or not. I also heard him getting up and going out the back door to smoke. I thought he could not sleep because of being upset about our decision regarding Gladys.

But I learned during future visits that Marell had trouble relaxing enough to sleep. Only now do I think about all the reasons why he may have been so tense. He knew that his family loved him, but I'm sure he was wondering what did other people think of him. Did they judge him? Were they scared of him? Our visits inside the prison had been in confined circumstances, lasting for no more than an hour at a time. Marell knew exactly what to expect. There were no surprises.

I never mentioned to James that Marell seemed stressed out because I knew what my husband might have said: "Well, what do you expect? It will blow over. This is him getting out into the world." But I worried that Marell seemed just too nervous.

Still, I don't want to make it sound like Marell's home visits were negative for him or us. They weren't, especially when he was here to celebrate special occasions, like my birthday. The girls and James had wanted to surprise me. But with getting everything together, they had to tell me about preparations for my party.

Kesia had sent out the invitations, mentioning that there would be a surprise visitor. So when our guests arrived, they immediately questioned, "Where is he?" "Has Marell got here yet?" This was my birthday party, yet I did not mind that all the attention seemed to be on him. Matter of fact, my biggest birthday present was having Marell come home to see more of his family and many of the important people in his life.

When James called to let us know that they were around the corner, we all made our way into the front yard to greet Marell. I hugged him first, then my mother took over. She had flown in from Texas just for this celebration. She's not a big person, but she's known for her great big hugs. "Ella hugs," we call them. She hugged Marell so hard for two or three minutes that she nearly squeezed the breath out of him. Several dear friends drove up just to give Marell more great big hugs, even though they did not plan to stay for the party. Then I whisked him to the back yard where Devon was the first to grab him. Devon and his mother had never stopped going to see Marell, though they had had little time with him lately.

James, Kesia, and Sidnee had decorated the backyard with birthday balloons and tents, and hung a birthday sign on the side of the house. Kesia had also hired a friend of hers from college who was a DJ and a professional photographer. He captured pictures of Marell, Kesia, and Sidnee enjoying one another as if no one else was there.

What a party! When time came to sing "Happy Birthday," James, my mother, and the children joined me standing around the cake table. They told me to make a wish and blow out the candles, and I wished for this happiness to always last. Then I began to cry. It was my first birthday celebration with all three of my children with me since 1995. Each of girls reached over and kissed me. When I expressed how happy I was that Marell was with us, he smiled and said, "I will always be here for you. I will never leave you." Then he kissed me too.

I was the proudest, happiest momma that day. I did not want this joy to end, especially for Marell. He had been his old self and the highlight of the party. He had marveled the crowd with his smiles and perfect conversation, talking to every person, noticing something special about each one. Relatives and friends were still visiting until he headed back to his other home that afternoon. I hoped that this memory would linger in his heart like it would in mine.

Holidays had been a problem for me while Marell was away, but in 2011, I felt like celebrating again, for real. We knew that Marell would miss dinner on Thanksgiving since it falls on a Thursday. But I always plan for leftovers with a few more dishes for Sunday dinner, when Marell would have an overnight visit that weekend. Tina and her pre-teen boys would be also joining us. She had been a friend of Marell in school, and for some time now, she occupied his time from the beginning to the end of a visit. I also invited Devon to spend time with Marell and meet Tina's sons. All four seemed to get along well watching TV in the back room. Every now and then, I would hear Marell checking on them.

During the years Marell had been away in prison, I couldn't get into the Christmas spirit. I didn't do any decorating, so James took care of whatever got done. We had an eighteen-inch high artificial tree that sat in a gold flowerpot. James would take it out of its storage box, saying, "Here goes the Christmas bush." I saw it as our Christmas *tree*. It was as much as I wanted. After the holidays were over, James would put it away until the next year.

But in 2011, I felt the Christmas spirit for the first time in sixteen years, and because Christmas fell on a Sunday, the day of Marell's regular visit, he would be at home to celebrate with us.

About the second week of December, I purchased a real Christmas tree, seven feet tall and bigger than anything we'd ever had since Sidnee was born. James took out all our boxes of decorations, some that I had made and others we had bought. I selected red and gold as my colors to use that year, just like old times when my kids were little and would ask, "What colors are we doing this year, Ma?"

James hung lights on the windows and the doors. Together with the girls, we decorated the tree. I made Christmas stockings and hung them from the shelf on the entertainment center and put wreaths on the windows. We had many more decorations that year than ever before. I wanted everything to be extra special for Marell. I was sure he had missed the Christmas celebrations most of all.

Marell didn't have any trouble eating Christmas dinner. I wanted to please him so I welcomed Tina and her boys too. She and Marell appeared to be getting serious. There were going to be many more holidays like this one.

III

The Prison after Prison
May 29, 2012, to December 1, 2014

TWENTY-ONE

Parole

By the time I was sixteen and had been baptized, I went to church because I wanted to, not because my mother forced me to. I wanted to hear the word of God surrounded by family and community leaders. Church was a place for bonding and fellowship. It felt good to be there.

I tried to go to church every Sunday, even when Marell was home for visits and I had to leave him with James. I could see that Marell wanted to go too. He was a people pleaser, but about this, he wasn't just trying to please me. He wanted to go to church because it gave him peace to be there.

Marell's good behavior on home visits finally earned him this privilege in March of 2012. I was very emotional that Sunday, though I tried not to show it. I wanted to slip in without making a big deal, and I knew that Marell didn't want people fussing over him.

But that didn't happen. Many, many people came up and hugged him. Our minister joked, "Marell, your mother's smiling. You know any reason why she'd be smiling?" The young people Marell had grown up with also welcomed him back. After communion, I asked for prayer from the church that my son's faith would be strengthened, that he would want to get right with God. He had to want that more than I did.

I took pride in having Marell and my husband and daughters with me. We were whole again. I gave thanks because, now for certain, Marell was on the road home.

That wonderful day helped to keep my mind off some bad news that came my way the same month. I had been on pain management since my accident at work two years earlier. By the beginning of 2012, my back and right leg were causing me fierce pain that limited travel in a car to only a few minutes. So James would drive without me to Robeson Correctional to pick Marell up and bring him back. During Marell's visits, I'd be in my recliner or in bed. Even though I could barely walk the distance to the mailbox in our yard, I still felt I had to cook and clean for my family. But I did that with moderation. Cook a while, sit a while. And at work, I was walking around bent over.

Finally, I got an appointment with an orthopedic surgeon. "You are still going to work every day?" he said, like he was asking a question. Then he swung his chair around to face me: "There's only one thing that will help you: surgery." An MRI had shown that a disc was pressing on my sciatic nerve, and surgery could chip off a bit of that disc to give the nerve relief.

My first response was "No!" I didn't want to be away from work. I spent so much time at Spivey Rec Center that I called it my second home. The children and community needed me. Who would organize the youth programs and recreational sports that changed with each season? The adult programs that included trips to plays or shopping and lunches? I had administrative duties, made schedules, and was responsible for other employees. But it was what I did beyond my job description that I felt I couldn't take time away from. Every day, I tried to show the children and adults who came through my doors that they were special. So I routinely put in extra hours talking with a troubled youth or visiting a child's home or taking senior citizens on out-of-town trips. I hated to let them down, even though I was bent over with back pain.

I was determined to carry on, and even more important, I didn't want to be laid up recovering, just when Marell was getting ready to come home. We had known for a couple of years that the day set for his release was to be May 29, 2012.

"Well," the doctor said, "if you want to be in pain and possibly never walk again, it's your choice."

In the car on the way home, James declared, "Spivey Rec Center can get along without you for a while." With any luck, I would be completely well by the time Marell was home for good.

So on Tuesday, April 17th, I had outpatient surgery and everything seemed smooth sailing. Because James was caring for me, sometimes he could not leave to bring Marell from prison for his visit, but Marell was okay with that. He just wanted me to get better and called often to say, "I will soon be home to take care of you."

While I was recovering, I contacted Marell's parole officer to inquire about the process of a prisoner coming home. First thing she said was that she'd never encountered the mother of adult inmate ask about such. That surprised me, and I replied that Marell had family backing him so that this transition would be as positive as possible.

I was also surprised to find out that families received no instructions about what to expect when an inmate is released; we'd had plenty of instructions to prepare for Marell's home visits. The parole officer did say she would go over a list of requirements with Marell before he left prison, and I told her I wanted my own copy of that list. I wanted Marell to know that we were on the same page, that I knew what he was supposed to be doing, or not doing.

I was also shocked that Marell would have no particular kind of job training right before his release. And it wasn't just job skills that he would need. He'd had a few self-help courses in prison at Hoke and New Hanover, but I didn't think that was enough guidance for him to adapt to society after so long in prison.

By now, Marell had spent sixteen years without having to pay the rent or find health insurance. His work release had lasted only some months here and there, never for a long period of time. That was it as far as having to get up and put in eight hours of work a day. Even though he had to pay the Department of Correction for his transportation back and forth to the job site, he didn't know what it was to make car payments or maintain a car. Bad as conditions might be in prison when it was too hot or too cold, Marell wasn't the one who kept the lights on. Close as he came to paying bills was that time he got money from the DOC to help me with his collect calls. How could he or any ex-inmate start acting like a productive member of society if he was just tossed out to fend for himself on the streets?

When I ended my phone conversation with the parole officer, I told her that I wanted Marell to start work the day after he got out.

But she, and Marell, and I sadly knew that was not likely.

On that beautiful Tuesday, May 29, 2012, the sun shone through morning clouds. What beats all, my follow-up appointment with the surgeon was scheduled for that same day. James and I settled that he would stay home to receive our son while someone else took me to the doctor. A prison official was to drop Marell off during a time frame—not at an exact hour. With luck, I'd be home before he arrived.

My faith had never wavered while Marell was in prison, and before I left for the doctor appointment, James and I held hands and prayed in our living room. We thanked God for this moment and asked for strength to cope with the changes coming with Marell at home. Now, with him about to be released, my beliefs were even more clearly defined. I needed to be an example because Marell would be watching me. He had to understand that without the Lord, his release from prison would not have been possible. To encourage him, I had made a little sign, really no bigger than a card. On it I had drawn puffy clouds and a rainbow, and under the arch of the rainbow, I had written the words from Philippians 4:13: "I can do all things through Christ who strengthens me." Marell could put this sign up on a wall, but it was small enough to fold in half and fit in his wallet so he could pull it out to read whenever he needed motivation.

I was so edgy when I arrived at the doctor's office that I was shaking. He asked if that was caused by back pain, and I was not ashamed to say that I was trembling with excitement because my son, who had been in prison for over sixteen years, was coming home. Even though I knew this was supposed to be to a short examination, I asked the doctor to hurry. He looked at my incision, said it had healed, and told me I could pick up a prescription for pain on the way out. The surgery had been successful, and the doctor was confident that I'd experience relief, though he wanted me to have a prescription for pain, in case I needed it.

On the drive home, the closer I got, the more anxious I became. I didn't want to talk. I just wanted to focus on the son who had been away for so long, to hug him without worrying that he'd have to return to prison by a certain hour. Then James called to say that Marell had arrived, and a few minutes later, I was in our front yard. Marell was leaning on Tina's car, and James was on the porch, having a conversation with them.

I moved slowly getting out of the car and called out, "Marell LaTrek Williams!"

"What's up, Rosalind?" he shouted back, as he approached to help me. Calling me by my first name instead of "Ma" was something he had done from time to time while he was in prison. Normally I would have fussed about it, but that day, I did not want anything to ruin our reunion and great big hug. But after all our embracing, I noticed that Tina was putting some of Marell's things in her trunk.

"What's going on, Marell?" I asked as he followed me into the house.

"I know all you've done for me, Ma" he started out. "So me living with Tina will be the best thing for you because you need a break."

A break? From what? Marell always thought he could put things in way to swoop me into his thinking. But that day, it wasn't working.

Months ago, he had mentioned that after he got out, he and Tina would be looking for a house together. I did know that Tina had found a house-for herself, I thought-and that she had moved there with her sons. But I never thought Marell would move in with her the same day he was released from prison. Getting himself together, finding a job, that would be a task within itself, one that he could best do at home. Immediately I began to cry.

"You don't have a job. You have nothing. Nothing to give her or those boys. Why? Why are you doing this?"

"Ma, I am going to get a job and take care of what I need to." He said this in an unsure voice, trying to convince himself more than he was trying to convince me. Did Marell now foresee what I did? That a convicted felon, even one who's served his time and goes to church, will have trouble finding work?

Then it occurred to me. "Wait. You can't move in with Tina. Your parole address is here, with us." But Marell assured me he had that under control, that the paperwork was being changed.

He and Tina finished packing her car with some household items I had previously gathered to give him whenever he decided to join her. Apparently, that time was now. They sat with us for a while and chatted. Then they left.

I ranted and cried most of the night, and James listened. "Why wouldn't you tell him he needs to stay here?"

"That's your opinion," James answered. "He's grown now, and it's his decision. He needs to be on his own and take responsibility."

After all I had done for Marell, this is how he repaid me? How dare he let someone else come before his mother? How could he let me down this way? What was he thinking? How was he going to make it without us helping him?

But in my heart, I knew some answers to these questions. Marell's home visits had given him a taste of what life with us would be like. I wasn't naïve. He wanted to be free to be with Tina the way he wanted to be with Tina. He wanted his space to smoke. He didn't want me to keep up with his comings and goings. He didn't want me asking what have you done with your life today? He knew that at home there would be no lying around.

Over the next few weeks, Marell set things up with his parole officer. (Of course I had called her on May 29th, right after he pulled out of the driveway, to get full details about his changed address.) He had regular monthly appointments in her office, and a parole officer would also drop by his house unexpectedly, just to check that he was where he was supposed to be.

Marell made a practice of calling me mostly every night to share his daily plans, and I tried to see him every day. Either I drove to his house, or, once he got his driver's license in November, he drove to ours. With money that I'd saved and with a generous friend's gift, Marell was able to buy a car. He was getting used to freedom and doing the normal things we take for granted like going to the grocery store or to church most Sundays. He also started being a part of the boys' lives by driving them to school or football practice.

I was still fuming that Marell wasn't living at home, but tried not to bring that up. It was comforting to blame Tina for Marell's decision. Still, I was willing to do anything to help Marell build his new life, and so was James.

He and Marell had talked about working together ever since Marell had taken those business courses at Hoke Correctional. He was enthusiastic about the ideas and plans he had previously written up. And James wanted to show off his part-time lawn care business, which had grown tremendously while Marell was away. For me, the best part was that both of them seemed excited about this opportunity for fellowship.

Marell quickly got into a regular routine of working with James on the weekends and on weekdays, whenever James got out of his job with the schools early enough in the afternoon. Marell looked forward to the money he made to help pay his monthly $40.00 parole fee, contribute to household expenses, and have a little change in his pocket.

What I liked best about this arrangement were the opportunities for father-son talks. Sometimes I'd remind James to discuss with Marell being responsible or keeping consistent with his work. These conversations also allowed Marell to learn from James what it is to live with a woman because I realized that my son had never lived with any woman besides me and his sisters, and Sidnee was only four when he went away. His whole adult life had been spent locked up with other men. He really knew nothing about how to make a woman happy.

James was the only one who gave Marell regular work, though lots of folks had said, "Make sure you contact me when Marell gets out. I will see what I can do."

A minister who had a construction business had literally promised me that he would find something for Marell to do. But when I took Marell to meet with him, well, wouldn't you know it? That minister described the business as being slow and never called back.

A close friend who was a county commissioner stopped by the house one afternoon to ask how Marell was doing. This man was involved with a program that gave felons a fresh start. He even went so far as to write a reference letter for Marell and accompany him to one of the local plants where they actually spoke with a manager in charge of hiring. Marell thought this would be a sure thing because that man promised to contact him. It never did happen.

Then there was Marell's childhood friend who had stayed with us for several weeks during high school when he had problems in his own home. Now he owned a small business and had many contacts. Each time he had visited Marell in prison, he mentioned giving him a job when he was released. So, of course, Marell thought he had a friend who was going to help him. But this was another dead end, and one that really disappointed him.

Every avenue headed nowhere.

So it was refreshing when a suggestion came from my goddaughter. She had worked with an organization that provides networking for people who are down on their luck and looking for jobs. Through this group, she had heard about Vocational Rehabilitation.

I presented the idea of VR to Marell. He was interested and made an appointment where an intake worker explained procedures to him and administered a standard VR test that would decide if he qualified for the program. That same day, she reported that the test revealed Marell had a lot of anger and wasn't able to stay focused. If there was a specific diagnosis that enabled him to get help from VR, it was never conveyed to me. I was just relieved that Marell had been approved for help and was going regularly to the VR office for job coaching, putting together a résumé that sort of thing.

But this was not a quick fix. Marell became agitated at VR's slow process and complained that a job wasn't coming fast enough. He also felt the VR caseworker suggested jobs that were beneath his qualifications. Dishwashing for only three hours a day at minimum wage. Part time trash collection. KP at Fort Bragg. Working the early morning shift at a fast food restaurant. I tried to persuade Marell, "At this point, take anything. A job is a job," and he needed one.

What he wanted was a position in communication technology, a field he had taken courses in and enjoyed so much while he was on work-release at New Hanover County Correctional. But when he applied for jobs in this field, he received few positive responses. When he did go on an interview or two, he never was called back.

"Just because you have a piece of paper that says you have a certain skill doesn't mean you're really qualified," I told him, "especially in a field that changes so fast."

Marell was trying to find a job, and my mother was retiring from hers: thirty-seven years teaching business education in high school. Naturally, my siblings and I were planning a celebration dinner for her in Texas.

Since Kesia, Sidnee, and James would not be coming, my family suggested that Marell should join me. The party would allow him to take a breather from job-hunting for a few days. Plus, he could be with family members that he had not seen while he was away. He was especially eager to see my sister Karen and her children Corey and Taliya. Marell had kept in close contact with them while he was in prison, even though they had never traveled from Texas to visit him.

The dinner was scheduled for November 24th, five days before Marell's six-month parole ended. There was a process he could go through to finish up a few days early, but there was also a problem. He had missed paying a month or more of his fees and his case could not be closed out until he paid up. Did that make Marell mad! He was adamant that he was not going to pay. He said he had already paid his debt to society with all those years in prison.

I was not at all sympathetic with his argument. "There are rules and regulations," I reminded him, "the law is the law." This was not the time for him to rebuke the system. When he was no longer on parole, then he could write a letter to a legislator or the Department of Correction. "Fight the system after you pay," I said.

Marell had put himself in this predicament, but he knew he had a family who could pay his fees for him when so many parolees do not have the money or the family to help them. Forty dollars a month may not seem much to most people, but if you've just left prison and don't have a job-don't even have the money to pay for gas or carfare to get to a job interview-forty dollars is a fortune.

So I went against my principles that Marell should take responsibility for his own bills. I paid his fees because I was determined that he should be at my mother's celebration. My father bought his airplane ticket, and he flew to Texas, arriving the night before the dinner.

How free Marell must have felt, to get on a plane, no longer controlled by the Department of Correction, no longer an inmate who had to get back to the prison at 5:00 in the evening or the parolee who had to check with a parole officer. He was out prison for real and part of our family again.

TWENTY-TWO
After Parole

At my mother's retirement party, I understood why Marell and his cousin Corey had been talking on the phone so much; they had put together a little surprise skit to begin the celebration.

"Good afternoon, everyone," Corey began, "how great it is that so many of you took time from your busy schedules to celebrate with us today."

"Celebrate what?" Marell said. "You mean Granny?

"Yeah, man! Granny!"

"So what did she do?"

"She has been teaching all of our lives." And that was so true. As long as those cousins had been alive, my mother had been a teacher.

"Why would we celebrate that?" Marell asked, in order to give Corey the chance to say, "Man! That is an honor. First she had to put up with us,"—"us" was my mother's eleven grandkids—"and then she went to school and put up with some more knuckleheads." Everybody laughed.

"Oh, yeah," Marell agreed.

"And that is why we are celebrating. I'm Corey."

"And I'm Marell. And we welcome you."

Marell's presence at my mother's retirement party gave me such joy, and then, a couple of months later, we had a celebration for him. All those years he'd been in prison I had said, "You'll be out by the time you turn thirty-five. You can still get married and have children. It won't be too late for you to enjoy life." Now here he was, on January 14, 2013, celebrating his thirty-fifth birthday. He was feeling good. We all were.

But if I'd learned anything walking down this long road with Marell, it was that good feelings didn't last.

I saw that he was getting more and more frustrated about finding a job. He would check in with the VR counselor, hoping that she would have some good leads. But weeks went by without any contact from her, and he felt she was not doing her job. I advised him not to give up, to search for a job on his own. When he did, he would be told, "We'll call you back." But no one ever did call back. He wondered if that was because he always checked "yes" to that question on an application: "Have you ever been convicted of a felony?" He said he wasn't going to be honest anymore, he was going to check "no," but I convinced him that he had to tell the truth. It would be worse for him to lie and then get found out through a criminal background check.

Marell also became discouraged working with James, who did not agree with some of his son's new ideas. James was old school. His way was the best way for him, and he expected Marell to speed up and get more accomplished in a given length of time. This was probably the hardest, hottest, outdoor physical labor that Marell had encountered in a long time, maybe since he was on the trash crew on North Carolina highways during one of his work release jobs. Not that Marell lacked a work ethic, but no one could match James Curtis Williams in his ability to work out in the sun. And Marell had more and more activities with Tina and the boys. He wanted to take a break on the weekends, especially if he had found odd jobs during the week. Eventually, the working fellowship dwindled between father and son, but if James was ever in a bind over a certain job, he'd still ask Marell for help, and he willingly stepped up.

Once parole was over, Marell had no set time to be in and no officer coming around to check at his home. When he lost that structure to his life, things changed. His calls to me slowed up so I found myself contacting him. His visits during the week were fewer. He appeared to be staying to himself, that is, away from James, me, and his sisters. His time was spent with Tina and the boys, and when he visited us, he came with her. If I wanted to have any private conversations with him to inquire about job possibilities and applications, I would call him into my bedroom. This would be my opportunity to give him a piece of change, which I did normally every chance I could, and to find out if he needed any personal items. I'd often buy toiletries and supplies for him and sometimes for the boys. If they needed some contribution to their household, I made it.

One thing I knew and respected was that Tina took care of Marell. She kept a clean house and always had plenty of food. So though I felt some neglect, I welcomed the fact that he had a home and wasn't with negative company. I knew what could happen if he fell in with some old acquaintances.

Early in 2013, one of his closest friends, Charles, was shot dead. He and Marell had gone to high school together, and Charles had also spent time in prison. I often accepted collect calls from him when his family could not afford them. No matter how many times I would tell Charles that this would be the last time I would accept his collect call, he would call again, and promise again to pay me when he got out. "You can repay me by not returning to the situation that put you in prison," I would say.

On the day of Charles's service, I took a picture of Marell and Kesia gathered together with three neighborhood friends. They were standing in front of the funeral home, their eyes puffed and red from crying. I thought of how they used to mingle together in the neighborhood when they were younger. None of them had a clue then how their lives would turn out, and Marell went into in a slump for weeks after the incident.

Even though I still believed Marell decided to move in with Tina too soon, his situation with her did take some worries away. She and her boys played a big part in Marell not turning to the streets. I could see him maturing and taking responsibility. I was proud that he had taken on the male role with the boys, not to replace their own father but simply to be a positive influence in their lives. He involved them in recreational football and brought them to Spivey Rec Center where I got to show Marell off, and he had a chance to see my job first hand. Marell also brought Tina and the boys to our family's gatherings. So when he asked to invite them to Sidnee's graduation from the University of North Carolina at Greensboro, I thought, why not? The more the merrier.

This was my busiest time of year at work because I had to line up the speakers and trips for summer campers. Normally, I would have started that in February, but I had gotten behind. During the months following my back surgery, I had leg pain worse than anything I'd experienced before, not post-op pain but something new, severe nerve pain in my right leg. According to the surgeon, that wasn't supposed to happen, and he stipulated that I could not stand or sit more than forty-five minutes to an hour. Whenever the pain got too bad, I would have to change my position. I couldn't drive long distances any more, so I couldn't take the kids on their field trips. On one occasion, when I should have taken them to a game in Charlotte, another employee had to drive them.

Still, I only missed work when I went to a doctor's appointment for shots in my back. I worked on summer plans for the rec center, even though that meant putting in overtime before taking off on Friday for Sid's two-day graduation events. That morning I packed snacks, sandwiches, and drinks. We probably would go out to dinner after her department ceremony, but bringing food still helped us save money.

James, Kesia, and I arrived at the auditorium mid-afternoon, early enough to get good seats for ourselves, Marell, Tina, and the boys. Late that night, my mother, my sisters Sheri and Andrea and her two children arrived in Greensboro from Texas. We were one big happy family. Next morning, at the Greensboro Coliseum, my former supervisor, "B.," and his wife joined us just as the prelude music started. They were like family now, though "B." had left Spivey many years earlier. I will always be grateful to him for his understanding and kindness when Marell got in trouble.

The ceremony was not long, and when it was over, I wanted to walk with everyone to the back of the coliseum where the graduates were filing out. I wanted to greet Sidnee and catch her laughing with her friends and boyfriend and take their pictures. But I just couldn't do it. Even walking with a cane, I couldn't move fast enough or take that many steps. So I sat down on a stone bench, under a tree, by myself for what seemed to be the longest time, just waiting. I looked for them this way and that. But they were back there, taking pictures and laughing, and I was crying because I couldn't be with them.

Still, to have seen Sidnee walk across that stage and get her diploma made this a proud and pleasing day, even though I couldn't participate fully. And I know how happy Marell was finally getting to see one of his sisters graduate. "My little sis," he said, smiling with pride.

Monday morning came too quick. I had not recuperated from the busy, exhausting weekend. My back and right leg were acting up. I didn't feel like going to work, but I refused to take another day off. I had gotten used to working through pain because I felt nothing could go on at Spivey without me. So I patted myself on the back for showing up, and by noon, all of the pre-planning for summer camps was complete. I felt pretty good about that. Little did I know this was going to be my last day with a job that I had loved for over twenty years.

After lunch I was called to the central administrative office to meet with the director. But this meeting would be not to praise me for how diligent I had been or to tell me how much I was appreciated for my hard work.

"We've known each other for twenty years," the director began, "so this is nothing personal, just business." Then he handed me a letter stating that my physical limitations forced him to offer me a choice: resign and file for medical retirement, or be terminated because I could no longer fulfill all of my duties. I had sixty days to make a decision that would affect the rest of my life.

This unexpected announcement devastated me. I had dedicated years to serving the people at Spivey. I had come in bent over many, many days and given my all. No matter what I decided, my contribution to that community was over. I immediately felt lost, without a purpose. For the first time, I realized how much of my self-worth was tied up with my career. Suddenly, my worth was gone.

Retirement was supposed to be a happy occasion, something to look forward to. Well, it wasn't going to be that for me. James tried to ease my worries over our finances. He knew that I always wanted to get all our bills paid on time, and he assured me that we still could do that. But how? Without my salary? Sidnee saw my despair, and said to me, "Ma, you have paid your dues. It's your time to rest."

James and my children tried to uplift me with positive words, but I was so overwhelmed with emotion that I shut down, just as I did when Marell got in his trouble. Along with suffering more physical pain, I withdrew from my family. Sometimes I wouldn't see Marell for days. I knew he was routinely filling out applications and even had a few interviews, though nothing ever came of them. He needed my encouragement, but I was so depressed I could barely give it. I was stationed in my house without the energy for anything but appointments with doctors.

Time was getting short for me to make a decision. May turned into June, and by the end of that month, my doctor approved me for medical retirement. And that's what I did.

My life's work was over. What was I supposed to do with myself when I got up every day? Why should I bother to get up every day? I couldn't even cook and keep up the house like I used to. James was continuing to do well with his job. My girls had recognized careers in their fields. Sidnee had begun teaching English in a Greensboro public middle school. Kesia was a legal aid attorney. They did something meaningful for the community each day. What could I do? I became more and more depressed.

Sometimes, when you're feeling sorry for yourself, life becomes so cloudy that you can't see clearly. And what I couldn't see then was that Marell was feeling the same emotions I was. What was he supposed to do with himself when he got up every day? Why should he bother to turn in another application for a job? Little odd jobs, like one painting with an acquaintance, had led to two roofing jobs before the call he always got. If my feelings of self-worth had disappeared along with my career, how must he have felt?

Now, when I look at Sidnee's college graduation photo album, I question what Marell was thinking under all his smiles. He seemed so happy. I wonder, was he really? Was he thinking that now both of his sisters had completed college, but he had not?

I had pumped him up by saying that at thirty-five, it would not be too late for him to start a family, and in his way, he had. But at the age of thirty-five, can anyone build a career, look forward to a pension? There would be no retirement party like the one we'd had for my mother in Marell's future. I see that now.

But on the day of Sidnee's graduation, all I had seen were my three children. They belonged to me and James. I never rated their degrees or qualifications. They were equal to me and to each other. I loved them each unconditionally.

Still, I am sure Marell was feeling that he had let himself and his family down. I understand that now, but then, my emotions were going haywire, and it took Marell to snap me out if it.

I had been out of work for several months, and I needed help with some housework. Early one morning, I called on Marell, but it had taken him all day to get to the house, and when he finally showed up, Tina and two of her sons had joined him. How was he going to get any extensive work done while they were waiting? Just another something to agitate me and make me cry.

Back pain had forced me to lie down most of the day, so after opening the front door for them, I went straight back to bed. Marell followed me, inquiring what he needed to do.

Instead of answering, I snapped, "You wait until the day is almost over and then you come with your family. How are you supposed to get anything done now? Just forget it."

"Ma, tell me what I need to do. I'm here now." He tried his best to get me to explain what I wanted done, but I lit into him about staying consistent, turning in résumés, and finding a job. He hadn't really slacked off, I knew that, but I was rambling, needing to find fault because he had disappointed me. I was in my own bad place, without work, so I criticized him for not beating the sidewalk every day when I should have understood how bad he felt without a job and getting rejections all the time. Playing this conversation back in my mind, I hear myself talking to a little child. I was full of my own unhappiness, and I didn't pay attention to my tone.

Marell turned to walk out of my room. Then, abruptly, he turned back and stood close to the end of my bed. This swift movement caught my attention. When Marell got mad, he balled his fists. He had done that from the time he was little, when he wanted to say something, yet dared not. This day his fists were tightly balled, but his words came out, and in a raised voice. "You are gonna have ta stop treating me like this. I am a grown man, Ma. I am tired of you treating me like a child. I am trying hard to please everybody-you, Pops, and Tina. It's hard, Ma. You gotta stop." Speaking to me in that tone was a rarity, and he kept on: "Sometimes I do not know if I am going or coming. I try to do everything you ask of me, and you act like you do not appreciate it and treat me like I'm a kid. I am not your little boy anymore. You don't need to hold my hand."

I sat up in my bed, my eyes full of tears, knowing immediately that what he said was true, but I was not able to respond. Marell had never spoken those words before, and he had never spoken to me with that tone. I was crushed, embarrassed.

I thought to myself, "Shame on you, Rosalind. Why do you make him feel this way? There is no excuse!" My head dropped down. I couldn't look at him because he had tears in his eyes. I realized how much I had hurt him, and I worried about how my words might affect his mental state. Each one of us—Tina, James, me—had different hopes for him. The stress of our expectations could break him down.

Soon I found the words to say, "I am so sorry I made you feel this way. I will work on changing. I do love you."

When Marell left the room, he was not angry any longer, just sad. Soon I heard the front door close. I felt so small and unattached to my son.

Marell and I spoke on the phone later that night, his usual phone call with me. He never did hold a grudge, but I was still crushed and guilty about the way that I had behaved.

TWENTY-THREE

Free at Last

I became a mother at a young age, and from that moment, I wanted to be a good mother and to make my own mother proud. She had stamped in me her faith in God and her beliefs: Speak truthfully. Your word is your bond. Respect yourself, your family, other people, and God. Take responsibility for yourself and what you do.

I wanted these ideals to be important to my children, too. Over and over I would tell them, "Be a leader, not a follower. If you are right, I'll follow you to the end. If you are wrong, I cannot stand with you. There will be consequences."

Marell had often let me know in his letters from prison, even when he was in the hole, that he'd never forgotten his foundation though he had chosen a different path. Right before he came home, he wrote his last letter from prison. This was on Mother's Day, my most important day of the year.

> Hey Mom,
> What sup!
> I just wanted you to know you really do mean the world to me and I thank you for the morals, values, and capabilities you instilled in me.
> Me and you grew up pretty fast together (mother-son/bestfriends). As a child, you opened my eye to a lot early and even though that may not have been what you wanted, it was what the "Lord" saw fit for you to teach me because only he knew my journey. Those things you taught me were the deciding factors that got me thru. Looking back, I admire you so much that your determination became mine. I've always seen your bigger picture and it will always be my goal. In my haste, I tripped and stumbled early along the way. I made a mistake, but you pushed on, not leaving me behind. Thank you for enduring my hardships, embracing me unconditionally, and being my guiding light thru

the darkness. I'm so proud of you!! And all I want to do is to make you proud. I will.

Marell's words meant all the world to me. Never did I question whether I had been a good mother, even when he got in his trouble, and a longtime friend told me, "Hold up your head and don't be ashamed!" What? Ashamed? I was not ashamed, because shame is what you feel when you've done wrong, and I knew I had done everything in my power to raise Marell right. I had spent hours in the corner crying then, but what I felt was deep sorrow, never shame.

But that day when Marell stood at the foot of my bed, I said to myself, "Shame on you, Rosalind." I felt *shame* because I had done wrong.

As I think back on my mistakes, I blame them on a mother's instincts to protect her children and make them happy. The mother in me wanted to help, but I had to learn when helping wasn't helping. How could Marell fully accept responsibility when I had taken care of so many things for him? I used to think that he would swoop me into his reality, but I realized that just as often, I was swooping myself in, especially when I felt he needed me. It felt good to be needed, and sometimes I went against my principles to make him happy.

Like paying his parole fees. "You did what?" I asked myself. On which day of the week was I being the mother who let him be an adult and pay his own bills? On which day was I the one who was sorry for him and wanted to make him feel normal? And what was normal anyway? Giving him clothes and shoes like his friends had? Or letting him go without unless he took odd jobs that he did not want in order to pay his way? Why had I acted like he was frozen in time, still my high school son, and me, the mother who needed to guide him?

"I am not your little boy any more. You don't need to hold my hand." Marell's words had been powerful, and so had mine. I questioned how I would go forward. I would have to think about what I said and how I said it. He did not need my nagging. He was grown. He was handling his own business. I needed to accept that.

Nothing was going to be the same again. I knew my habits of trying to keep up and control Marell had to stop. This would be a process, and I would work diligently to make Marell independent.

Late in the fall of 2013, Marell rekindled a friendship with a high school classmate whose mother ran a center for former addicts. She suggested that Marell become qualified to be a peer specialist in her program by taking courses and a test online. She even agreed to pay for these.

Marell completed a forty-hour course and received his first certificate. Then he attended a seminar, passed an online test, and earned another certificate. He was so proud of what he had learned. When he discussed it with Kesia and Sidnee, he sounded like he was now on their professional level. Since he was qualified to aid in the recovery of substance abuse clients on a small scale, I was expecting him to work at the center. I thought this was the purpose of the coursework he had taken, and so did Marell. But after several months, he realized that there would be no job placement for him, at least not there.

Why would that woman have paid for him to take coursework if she didn't have anything for him, I wondered. The old me would have gone to her and asked just that. But I didn't. I was working at letting Marell handle his own business, not stepping in and treating him like a child. And Marell had no luck when he applied for jobs with the county Mental Health Department. Could it have been because he had a record? I always thought so. I was more upset about this than Marell was because he had enjoyed taking those courses.

Marell's hopes of becoming a peer support specialist faded, and near the end of the summer of 2014, he spent time researching different trucking schools. I thought that this was just another idea that would change with the seasons. But I didn't express my opinion. I was learning to keep my mouth shut.

A couple of Marell's acquaintances had gone to trucking school, and they told him that some companies gave grants for training, and after the student completed it, he would be hired. This would be helpful because Marell did not have the money to pay for training. One day he was at my house when I overheard his phone conversations with two or three different companies he'd applied to. One conversation especially broke him down.

The hiring manager had received Marell's application and seemed eager to have him start. But there was that question Marell had not answered. "I would rather meet with you face to face and explain," Marell said. "Well, I tell you what," the man said, "we will get back with you after my boss views your application." Marell hung up and said to me, "It has happened again." I knew just what he meant.

Weeks later when I thought the trucking school possibilities had ended, Marell learned that a company out of Atlanta would pay for his six to eight weeks of training. He would have to pay for his meals and a place to stay while he was at the school, and then he'd work for partial pay for a certain length of time. After that, there would be a guaranteed job in his future.

I was a little leery about all this at first, yet I remembered what I had been working on. I tried not to judge, and I didn't ask about this guarantee of a job, or about him going to Atlanta by himself, or about the people he'd be rooming with. Instead, I switched into my new mode: "Marell, if you think this is good idea, we'll support you in it."

But I did suggest that he contact his counselor to see if VR could sponsor his room and board. The counselor spoke back and forth with the trucking company and resolved that the VR would pay Marell's living expenses while he was at the school. So James and I helped him to prepare to leave. I purchased a new suitcase that would hold his clothing for ten days or more. He was excited, packed, and ready to go any time he got the word.

When he got instructions to leave before Thanksgiving, I did not like that this schedule messed with family time, and I didn't keep that opinion to myself. James, as always, said, "Let him go and be a man." But, when Marell's departure date was delayed until two Fridays *after* Thanksgiving, was I happy!

While Marell was making his plans to go to Atlanta, he stayed away from the house. If he did visit, he'd come in and go right out. A couple of times when he called, he mentioned being sick. I took that lightly because he gave me no specific symptoms. Looking back, I think he was concerned about worrying me. And maybe he didn't want to make a big deal of how he felt because he didn't want anything to ruin his plans. Because I was still distracted by back pain and my loss of productivity, I did not notice changes in him.

On the Saturday morning before Veterans Day, I went to a youth football game. That particular Saturday was sunny and a little windy but warm enough that I only needed a light jacket. I was surprised and pleased when Sidnee showed up at the beginning of the game. As it was ending, Kesia arrived, and when we were leaving, we saw Marell approaching us from the parking lot. My children hadn't made a plan for us to be together. It just happened, and I was beaming to have the three of them at my side. So of course I handed my camera to a friend to capture the moment with our picture.

I figured Marell must be feeling somewhat better to be out and around like that, but next week, he mentioned that he couldn't keep anything down, and his stomach hurt badly. He never did like to go to the doctor, and he had missed a regular appointment at the clinic. Because he was low on blood pressure medicine, he was taking it sparingly.

I begged him to go to the doctor, and when he did, she said his blood pressure was out of control. She put him on stronger meds, but what really scared me was she said that if he had waited a week longer to see her, he might not be here.

After that, I checked on Marell daily and went to see him if he could not get over to the house. He was still sick, but playing down his symptoms. The only way I got details was through Tina. He insisted he was okay. All he wanted to talk about was going to Atlanta after spending Thanksgiving with Tina's family.

Marell thought he was a chef, and Tina and the boys boasted about his cooking. Matter of fact, he planned to prepare the food for her family's Thanksgiving dinner. He even bragged on a new recipe for baked potatoes that he wanted to fix, and I told him he could make them for us on Monday evening.

It is a Williams family ritual to have a second Thanksgiving dinner the Sunday following. Food is always left over, and it tastes even better than it had on Thursday. So after church, I came home and prepared our leftovers. Marell and Tina would be coming by, though they would not be staying long because he was still not feeling his best.

When they arrived, I fixed them both plates, but Marell picked through his food. He thought he had a little indigestion and asked for a coke. With the symptoms he described, I agreed this would be good idea. Possibly he just needed to burp.

When Marell finished eating, I expected him and Tina to leave because she wanted to check on the boys, who were at home alone. But Marell didn't take her up on that. When James came in after working on yards—something unusual because he never does get back so early—we all sat in the living room. It was wonderful, all of us being together, knowing that next weekend Marell would be in Atlanta training for his job.

Marell went to the kitchen often. He nibbled food left on the table, which I took as a sign that he felt better. Every time he passed the chair where I was sitting, he leaned down to kiss my cheek. Marell often showed affection when greeting or leaving me, but this was strange. Then, out of the blue, he announced he'd pay for me to get a new kitchen with his first paycheck from the trucking job. I laughed and said, "Boy, you're going to need all that and more just to get yourself together."

And then, what was really crazy, he talked about how he wanted to be buried in a cardboard box. "A cardboard box? Why are those words coming from your mouth?" I asked. This was nothing I wanted to discuss. James asked Marell to talk about something else, and reluctantly, he changed the subject.

That afternoon had surely been different, but so nice in many ways. When Marell and Tina finally announced they were ready to go, I was still worried about Marell's complaint that his chest was hurting, but I stuck to my theory that he had indigestion and sent him off with a bag of goodies and his favorite, a whole pecan pie.

It was pure dark when James and I walked them out. Marell lingered in the yard making small talk. "You need to go and check on the boys," I said, while I slid a piece of change in his bag. "Take something for that indigestion when you get home," I reminded him. I looked forward to seeing him the next night when he would return with his special baked potatoes.

"You are my heart," Marell said, and he hugged me so tight. I pulled back and looked at him: "That's what I always say to you."

He laughed, "Well you are, Ma." Then he and Tina pulled out of the driveway. For some reason, she was driving. Marell was in the passenger's seat and waved out the window until they disappeared around the curve.

I leaned on James's shoulder and said, "Marell acted like he did not want to leave us." James agreed.

I called Marell later that night. Tina and the boys had already gone to bed, but he was sitting up because of that indigestion. We ended the conversation by telling each other, "I love you."

Six hours and twenty-three minutes later I received a phone call. One of Tina's boys was screaming. Marell was not breathing. Foam was coming from his mouth.

"Call 911," I yelled into the phone, but by the time I said that, Tina had already made the call and an ambulance was on the way.

When James, Kesia, and I got to the hospital, an emergency room doctor said the words no parent ever wants to hear: "We tried everything we could; we could not bring him back." The cause of death, heart failure due to complications from hypertension.

Marell's funeral services were too painful for me to describe. All I can say is that the following weeks were dark ones for the Williams family. After the service, people kept coming to our home morning and night to pay their respects, searching for something to say, something to do for us. They meant well, but we needed to put ourselves back together.

My mother and some of my other relatives stayed with us. We had never seen each other in such a state of grief. We were like strangers that we didn't recognize. I couldn't think. I couldn't eat. I couldn't sleep. Much later, I realized that James and the girls felt I'd pushed them away when I thought I had embraced them. We were tiptoeing around each other, searching for words of comfort because there was so much pain within our hearts.

I needed my family and God desperately. Many verses in the Bible brought me peace, especially this one from Psalms 61:2: "When my heart is overwhelmed, lead me to the rock that is higher than I." Over and over I repeated out loud, "The Lord makes no mistakes." I never questioned why. It was His plan.

All those nights while Marell was away at prison, I had asked the Lord to bring him safely home. I spoke my prayers loud and clear for God to hear: "Keep Marell from danger and harm so that he can come back home to me. Amen."

And that is what the Lord did, but he made no promises about the next phase of Marell's life.

Shortly after the services, James, Kesia, and Sidnee decided that we needed to go away for the Christmas holiday. It wasn't easy for me to agree, but my girls explained how we could celebrate Marell's life on the ocean waters of Galveston, the city where he was born. So we did, and my parents and siblings joined us there. Kesia and Sid wrote Marell's name in the sand, and we all watched the waves pull it away.

Sidnee suggested that as soon as we returned home, I should pull out the book that I had started about Marell right after his arrest. I had wanted to write about the day he was born and when he was a little, mischievous boy. Then he got charged with murder, and I didn't know how to connect these two sons in my memory. "Writing might be what you need to bring you closure," Sidnee said, and I accepted her advice.

Writing was helpful. I didn't want to forget my memories, but in my grief, they were often too painful to remember. Then James found a way to redirect my attention and keep me busy with some renovation to our home. After living in the same place for twenty-seven years, some things were just overdue like a larger kitchen and a larger dining room. When Sidnee tagged in to remind me, "You know Marell wanted this for you," I was convinced.

I was mourning Marell, and there were days when I thought I would collapse under that burden and the chaos of renovation. My home was filled with boxes and dust and strangers coming and going for nearly four months. But I was forced to get out of bed every day, to be in charge and guarding over something. That was good for me, though I didn't see it then.

By Mother's Day of 2015, the work was finished. As we dedicated our new dining room, sixty-seven friends and family members, who had seen us through our hard times, joined us for a meal. My mother and sister Sheri came from Houston and helped me put out a spread of fried and baked chicken, roast beef, pork barbecue and all sorts of side dishes—green beans, carrots, cabbage, mac and cheese, rice, hush puppies, and more. I had baked a coconut cake, a favorite of James, and other desserts.

The weather was gloomy that day. The official opening of hurricane season was still a month off, but tropical storm Anna was hitting the coast of North Carolina. Dark clouds hung over Fayetteville, and it rained on and off all day. By 3:30, our guests began to arrive, and at 4:00 sharp we circled around our big new oak table. Sheri began our ceremony of dedication and thanksgiving, thanking all our friends and family for their love and support over the last painful months.

Then James P., a dear friend, offered a prayer: "Please hold hands and bring your minds to Jesus," he asked. "We are grateful for the many blessing you have bestowed on us, for bringing us together today in this beautiful new room which is the heart of this house. The road we traveled to get here today is not the one we would have chosen for ourselves, Lord, but we thank you, and trust that you know what is best."

"Yes, Lord, thank you," someone said, and then another voice said, "Thank you," and others, "Thank you." "Thank you."

"You have brought us today to this place of love. Lord, the world can be cruel and harsh, but we ask you to bless this house and keep it safe as a refuge. We dedicate this room and everyone in it to you."

"Amen." "Amen." "Amen." Voices rose up from each part of the room.

Then James, my James, spoke. Tears rolled down his cheeks. He took a few seconds and slow breaths to compose himself before he said, "I'm going to get through this. I'm going to get through this," and after another deep breath, he spoke: "I want to dedicate this room to the memory of my son and name it Boone's Place."

James held up that wooden plaque Marell had made in ninth-grade shop class. I recalled the day Marell brought it home; he was so proud, though the letters were a bit crooked, and he hung it in his room above his window, and now, James said, "Anyone who comes into this room will be coming into Boone's Place."

Next Kesia surprised me by coming forward to say a few words: "My life has been turned upside down since Marell passed, but my family has become closer. I still have the last text that Marell sent me as I came out of court one day: 'Can't wait to see you in action.'"

Then Sheri spoke again, "As a sign of our gratitude for what each of you has done for us, it will be our privilege and pleasure to serve you your food."

I did not speak. I could not. But I took comfort in being able to prepare a meal for my friends and family, and in being able to serve it in Boone's Place.

By the next day, the storm had passed. The sun shone brightly. I felt proud of my son, and I knew he was smiling. I wanted him to remember what I had told him at the hospital as I held his lifeless hand, "I am here, always will be, and I will not let your life be in vain."

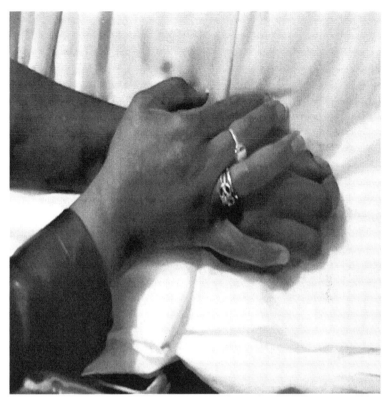

Figure 23.1. *Source:* **Rosalind Boone Williams**

When you were a baby, at birth I held your hand
And promised to love you forever
When you were a young child, I held your hand
And thought you would leave me never
As you became a young man, I still held your hand
And you reminded me you could hold your own
As God lifted you this day, I strongly held your hand
And promised that you were not going alone
You left with a part of me

Rosalind Boone Williams, December 1, 2014

Afterword and Acknowledgments

I have wanted to write a book since the day Marell got arrested. I thought writing about my son would help me understand how the child I raised became the man who got into deep trouble. But uncontrollable circumstances forced me to put that book aside for many years.

When Marell died, my younger daughter encouraged me to go back to this book. At the same time, I received a condolence call from Marell's high school English tutor, Pat Valenti. She had kept up with him during his early years in prison, and she knew that I had wanted to write about him. Pat and I met at Barnes and Nobles, caught up, and bonded over lunch while she reviewed what I had written.

I wanted to respect Marell, but I was still looking for answers. As Pat and I talked, I realized there was so much about him I didn't know. There were questions that I had never asked him, questions he never answered when I did ask, and things I really didn't want to know. Sometimes I did not know what he was thinking and feeling.

But I realized I knew what I felt and thought, and right then, an abrupt switch took place. It was not Marell's life that I wanted to write about but my life ever since that terrible February night in 1996. Just like that, I had a vision and a purpose: to guide and motivate others, especially other mothers, going through the pain, heartbreak, anguish, and complete change to their lives caused by having a child or relative in the prison system. I wanted those people to know that prison should make no difference in your love. And to those who have not shared this heartbreak, I hope you will understand what it takes to stand by someone who is in prison for years.

When I left Barnes and Nobles that day, I knew I was going to tell *my* story. My friendship with Pat and the book draft began to grow. Both were a little overwhelming because I was forced to re-live painful memories. Though I know some people may remember things differently, I present my memories as accurately as I remember them. Sometimes I have checked my memories, and many times I filled them out, by looking at the journal, photographs, and all sorts of documents that I saved for many years.

During the twenty months Marell was in jail, I kept a journal to record important names, dates, and events. Everything was changing so fast I needed to create some order in my life and the journal helped me do that.

Then there are Marell's letters and cards to me and his dad. I saved all of them. Why? I can't give a reason. Maybe I thought I would go back and read them to comfort my woes. I also kept all clippings from the newspaper about Marell's case and copies of my letters to and from prison staff-anything that I thought might help me help him. When I use one of Marell's letters in this book, I quote it exactly as he wrote it.

There were many more letters that family and friends sent to Marell. When he would be moved from one prison to another, or one cellblock to another, or when he was sent to the hole, he'd have to get rid of some of his personal possessions. He did this by putting things in a box that he sent home. Marell was a very orderly person, and he organized the letters he received, copies of his letters to prison officials, receipts, disciplinary forms, court documents, tax forms for his pay during work release-every piece of paper that had come his way.

Whenever I received one of his boxes, it would take days for me to open it. Just looking at that stack of papers inside felt invading, so I didn't read anything then. But I kept the boxes, just the way Marell had packed them up, because I could not let go of these tangible parts of his life. Now that I have read what is inside, I feel as if Marell gave me what I needed to tell my story.

Another way I checked facts for this book was by looking through my picture albums. I take my camera with me wherever I go and snap pictures at all family events and celebrations. Then I print and organize my photographs into albums that I dated and keep on a shelf.

Because I have wanted to be as honest and accurate as possible, on a few occasions, Pat and I have checked facts by looking at information that is part of the public record or on the North Carolina Department of Correction websites. Although I use the names of my immediate family members, I have changed the names of everyone else. I want to respect their privacy.

I never lost my zeal to share my journey, and people need to know that it is a long, long journey when you persist in loving and supporting your child in prison. I give thanks to everyone who helped me take one step after another on a long, rough road.

I am grateful first to the Lord for continuing to give me strength and faith. Through His grace and mercy all things are possible, and I rely on the New King James Version of the Bible to inspire and support me every day.

I am grateful to my husband, James, who loves me unconditionally and never put his pain ahead of my pain; he always had an encouraging word and stayed clear headed when my world was very foggy. James, I will love you forever.

I am grateful to my daughters, Rikesia and Sidnee, for not giving up on me and realizing how important motherhood is to me; to my mother, Ella Ruth Brown, who has influenced many of my beliefs and given me continued support; to my sisters Andrea and Sheri who became listening ears and helped with my creativity; to my dear friend Pat Valenti, who the Lord put in my life for a reason, and to her family who spent countless time and effort helping me complete this project; to Marell's friends, his coach, and our church members who cared for him, visited, wrote letters and sent him funds during his prison years; to the strangers I encountered on my path who showed compassion when I most needed it; to all who offered encouragement, who read drafts, and pushed me to complete this book because they knew how important it was. I thank you from the bottom of my heart for your prayers. There is no way for me to express how much your kind words and encouragement meant to Marell, to me, and to my family members.

About the Authors

By profession, **Rosalind Boone Williams** was the director of a municipal recreation center where she dedicated her career to mentoring youth. She is an avid amateur photographer and writer of poetry and short stories that express compassion for those in difficult situations. She derives daily strength through her belief in God, and her most important role in life is being a mother. That role has impelled her to publish this story. With it, she aspires to encourage others who have a child in the penal system and to enlighten those who have not experienced this life-altering circumstance.

Patricia Dunlavy Valenti is professor emerita in Department of English and Theatre at the University of North Carolina at Pembroke. She has published two biographies; she is honored that Rosalind invited her to co-author this memoir.